The Legend of Bushistotle

This book is a work of fiction. Names, characters, businesses, organizations, places, events, and incidents either are the product of the author's imagination or are used fictitiously. Any resemblance to actual persons, living or dead, events, or locales is entirely coincidental.

Copyright © 2005 Intercontinental Creative Ltd.
All rights reserved.
ISBN: 1-4196-0794-4

To order additional copies, please contact us.
BookSurge, LLC
www.booksurge.com
1-866-308-6235
orders@booksurge.com

The Legend of Bushistotle
History's Greatest Philosopher-Warrior-King

Steven Hanley

2005

The Legend of Bushistotle

It all started innocently enough, in a way that no one would have ever imagined: I was scrolling through spam from spammers who seemed convinced that my penis wasn't long enough despite the years I'd spent yanking at it in the darkness, when I happened upon a message from a Mrs. Irma R. Gorgonzola.

Now, if Irma R. Gorgonzola is not a fictitious-sounding name of the type so often used by spammers—why just today none other than Hercules Rubric sent me an invitation "to become a better man" (and ha-ha to that, I say)—then I don't know what is. But something piqued my interest about this email in a way that only about one in a hundred spammed emails does: she said she needed me *"urgente."* Indeed, her email header read like this:

From: Mrs. Irma R. Gorgonzola
Sent: Saturday, January 1, 2005 12:01 PM
To: Steven Hanley
Subject: URGENTE! Wee Knead a U!

Honestly, who could resist opening an email that proudly proclaims "Wee Knead a U," especially when penned by a Mrs. Irma R. Gorgonzola? Yes, one runs the risk of infecting one's computer, and perhaps one's entire household, with a virus (quite possibly cheese-borne, so beware), but I just had to see what she knead me a for. And it was a good thing that I did, because Mrs. Irma R. Gorgonzola had this to say:

Eye a am a dee a head a libarian a at a dee a Vatican a libary and a wee a knead a u services too a overlook a new a ancient manoscritto dat a wee find a inna dee a stacks a, and wee a tink it's about dee a famous warrior a, Bushistotele. Wee a unnerstand a dat a u is a—how a u a say a, "traduttore?"—of a ancient Greek a, and a all a of a our a ancient Greeks a here a is a dead. Canna u a please a help a?

Sincerely,
Mrs. Irma R. Gorgonzola
Head Libarian

Well a, dee a....

Wait! I don't talk like that! Let me start again!

Well, the first thing I noticed is that Mrs. Irma R. Gorgonzola was not, as one might have thought she should be, the "Librarian," but she claimed to be the "Libarian" without the "r," which instantly endeared me to her. For forty-odd years I'd been searching for a libarian who said libarian the same way I did—"libarian"—and finally I found one! Certainly that was not a mistake that a spammer would ever have made, I convinced myself, so this little endearment made me type out a quick response to Mrs. Irma R. Gorgonzola, asking her exactly what she kneaded of a me vis-à-vis this ancient manuscript. I especially wanted to know more about her claim that a new work had been found about Bushistotle, the greatest Philosopher-Warrior-King of Athens, and I daresay of all history, the truth about whom we moderns know so very little.

I wasn't expecting a fast response because a) I didn't really deep-down believe that there was a Mrs. Irma R. Gorgonzola, though I really wanted to find out; and because b) if there really was a Mrs. Irma R. Gorgonzola, it was Saturday, and I've never known an Italian to work on Saturdays; and because c) it was New Year's Day, and I figured that anyone named Mrs. Irma R. Gorgonzola either d) had a wicked hangover like I did, or e) was at Mass, since January 1 is a Holy Day of Obligation for us Catholics, fallen like myself or otherwise pious, forced as we supposedly are to celebrate the Circumcision of Christ by kneeling in a pew with our heads hung low in prayer rather than with our heads hung low in the toilet, which seems a much more appropriate place to celebrate anybody's circumcision to me, especially when it falls on New Year's Day: what a way to ruin a holiday.

But boy I was surprised! Not only was AOL working for a change, but I got an instant Instant Message back from Mrs. Irma R. Gorgonzola explaining exactly what she knead a me a for; to spare you the gore of her grammar, I'll summarize: the Vatican had just found a new work in their libary that purported to be the True Story of the legendary Bushistotle—not the tall tale spun by his official historian, Carolus Rovus, which unfortunately is how most people have come to know Bushistotle—that they wanted me to get started on translating right away, because based on my immodestly boastful website, wherein I falsely advertised that I was fluent in ancient Greek, they thought that I was perhaps the only person in the world qualified to do the job. I, naturally, agreed with their inflated opinion of myself and promptly accepted the assignment, because you have to admit if you're a translator that it's not too often you get an email from a Vatican Pooh-Bah saying that they want you to translate a newly-found ancient manuscript, regardless of how mangled that Pooh-Bah's English might be, or how more-than-mangled your own ancient Greek might be.

I took the first flight to Rome that I could: I barely had time to find my ancient Greek / modern American dictionary, which somehow I'd placed next to a 1998 Syracuse Yellow Pages that I just about never used since I don't live in Syracuse and never did, so it was a surprise to me to even find it there. In any case once I did I shoved my cats in a bag, left them at my mother's, and before she had the chance to refuse I darted straight to the nearest airport. I was glad when we arrived because Italy has always fascinated me, perhaps because whenever I go there they make me feel like an honorary Italian, even though my complexion is pasty, my eyes are blue, and what hair I have left that's not gray is conspicuously mousy-brown.

Vatican City, however, is different: very somber, and way too holy for me. Like its sister European mini-countries—Monaco, San Marino, Andorra, and Liechtenstein, altogether less than half the size of Rhode Island—the Vatican's number one export, besides dogma, is stamps, not wafers as you might expect, and the line to the post office seems endless. *Plus ça change*, I suppose, so I bought my postcards and sent them before I even set foot inside St. Peter's, to get it out of the way. Naturally, I lied: "Hi, Mom, having a great time, wish you were here." No, I didn't "wish she were here," and no, I wasn't "having a great time": my purpose for the moment was entirely scholarly, and her purpose was to take care of my cats.

In my last email exchange with Mrs. Irma R. Gorgonzola she had instructed me to enter through a side door, which I did. One knock, and I was whisked inside by a gaggle of ironclad nuns. Not the wrinkly pious type with overly-starched habits that the Vatican would like you to believe people convents all throughout Christendom, but the old-fashioned nasty Catholic-School type who pack holsters stuffed with steel rulers for whacking you across the knuckles on, just in case you get out of line. These black-robed dames with sensible shoes pushed me and shoved me down the hall—very tastefully painted, I might add, though I didn't really get time to stop and appreciate as much as I would have liked—until I found myself standing in front of a massive wooden door. Briefly I thought that maybe St. Peter was on the other side, but then I came to my senses and realized that St.

Peter was unlikely to be anywhere that I was, at least not at the very same time.

One nun, let us call her Sister Mary Subjugation for lack of a better (or more apropos) name, opened the door, and there sitting behind a massive desk was an even massiver woman, who could only have been Mrs. Irma R. Gorgonzola herself. Mrs. Gorgonzola was a buxom broad, to say the least, the kind you might expect to find on a spaghetti commercial with a very full plate, shoveling cheese. But she motioned the nuns to shove me right in which they did, and was very cordial about it despite the dust that was everywhere. So cordial, in fact, that we shared a couple of snorts of cognac just to get the mood going.

Having slept with a few priests myself I was unsurprised to find Irma's filing cabinet chock so full of such fine brandies, yet I was never one to turn down a decent drink, either. If nothing I'm nonjudgmental. Irma motioned the nuns to skedaddle, which they did, then she filled my glass and hers, which she held up as if beckoning a toast. I followed along, beckoning right back.

"Dank a u for a cumming," Irma said in her best proto-English, which sounded just like her emails, and was prone to double-entendre. "Wee a knead a u services. Chin-chin!"

"Chin-chin!" I chimed back, and we both guzzled our chalicefuls.

"U a wanna more?" Irma asked, smacking her lips.

"Well, if you insist," I said.

"Eye noa insist," Irma answered. "Only iffa u want."

"Well then I'll have one anyway," I said. "Otherwise, it'll go to waste."

"Dat's a my a teory, too," Irma said, and we toasted a second time. "Now a, down a to a business!" Irma pounded the back of an old leather chair that spit up a whirlwind of dust, some of which smelled like it had been there since Michelangelo started moistening up his very first roller. I gathered I was meant to sit there and did, and Irma waddled her way back behind her massive desk, tinkled a little bell. "Dat a bee for a Sister Naomi," Irma said. "She a find a dee a *manoscritto*."

Just then a side door opened and in shuffled Sister Naomi, who was a very old soul, indeed. As I watched her it struck me immediately that you never really meet a Naomi older than 28, most especially who are nuns, and even more most especially who are nuns at the Vatican: Naomis must all die young or something, so don't name your next daughter that if you want grandkids.

Nonetheless, more to the point: "Sister Naomi tell a u dee story," Irma said.

Sister Naomi approached me slowly, whispered in my ear, but what I heard was: "Achim sadoc abiud amon zorobabel."

Since that couldn't possibly be right, I asked, "What?"

"Achim sadoc abiud amon zorobabel," seemed to be the answer back.

I looked at Mrs. Irma R. Gorgonzola for an explanation.

"She a berry old," Irma announced, as if that was a surprise. "Old a peeples, dey a shrink, and dere a voices a shrink, too. Sometime, itta hard to hear a dem."

I nodded for lack of a better response, turned back to Sister Naomi, who went right on talking in her shrunken voice. Eventually, in what seemed to take as long as Sister Naomi had been alive—since early Christian times, best I could tell—I gleaned the story out of her. She started her tale by claiming that she had been born in the catacombs, and as unbelievable as that might seem to some, one good look at her convinced me. Skipping over the fifteen hundred intervening years of detail in the middle, she said that she had been a supporter of a different, more gender-friendly candidate in a past papal election, so she tried to rig the vote in his favor and as penance was given eternal cleaning duties in the libary. Zip past another 25 years of her everlasting life story and here she is, cleaning away in some of the more remote stacks of the Vatican Secret Archives, when bingo: a new manuscript, "right there next to the 1998 Syracuse Yellow Pages that they just about never use anymore," to borrow Sister Naomi's own words, reflated back from their shrunken size. Which of course makes it one of those intercontinental coincidences that nobody would believe if you told them, but that sends shivers down your spine when you think about it, because that's exactly where I had found my ancient Greek / modern English dictionary!

Irma reached under her desk, pulled up a big leather-bound volume, plopped it in front of me. Poof—more dust everywhere!—and Sister Naomi just sighed, took a can of Lemon Pledge out from under her habit and, pained as Sisyphus must have been, started dusting the furniture again.

"Diss a bee a it," Mrs. Irma R. Gorgonzola said. "Dee a *manoscritto*."

I flipped through a few parchment folios of the thing and I have to say that it was in pretty crappy shape, not only because the anonymous ancient writer's handwriting wasn't half as good as it should have been (though I'll stay mum on that because of my Greek skills), but because according to Mrs. Irma R. Gorgonzola, "Sister Naomi, she a spill a bottle of a Windex onna dee a whole a ding, just as a she a was a switching dee a—how a u a say?—interchangeable refill a nozzle."

Just at that moment Sister Naomi bowed her head in shame as well she should have, because her ill-fated encounter with one interchangeable refill nozzle had left a bluish-green blotch on just about all the pages that I was going to have to work through when I was trying to figure out what was written, never mind the residual smell of ammonia on the parchment that would burn my sinuses to no end. Then there were the usual smudges that are just about unavoidable when you have to keep on dipping your feather into what must have been a pretty huge vat of ink given the size of the volume. That you can sort of forgive the original author for, but Sister Naomi and the Windex fiasco really teed me off, because it was just plain clumsy.

I didn't have to get beyond page one of the manuscript to see what a true find it was, however. Imagine, those long-rumored dialogs among that greatest of philosophers, Bushistotle, plus his Athens Academy of Philosophy and Warfare sidekicks Cheneyon, Rumsfeldiavelli, Powellonius, Ashcroftus and Constantina, <u>had actually taken place</u>, and I was looking at the minutes! It makes your hair stand on end: world events were not as haphazard as they would appear in hindsight, and barring Sister Naomi—who can't read ancient Greek in the first place, which is why the Vatican emailed me *"urgente"*—I was the first person in millennia who was able to partake, albeit barely, of so much learning and erudition and wisdom, which learning, erudition, and wisdom, I might add, have had such a profound effect on the semi-recent history of the Western World even though it's all these thousands of years later. I guess you could say that had it not been for Bushistotle America would be a very different country today, never mind everyplace else. First of all we wouldn't have any of our beloved political institutions fashioned as they were in his image, and second of all we might not even have ever had the chance to live in a Democracy with a capital "D" because nobody else would have had the balls to spread it so liberally around the globe like he did. Just these little things that were probably no more than a blip in Bushistotle & Co.'s minds at the time have so profoundly affected how we live our lives today.

I flipped through a few more pages, just to see what I was up against. "I'm a uniter, not a divider," cropped up continuously, but of course Bushistotle, the most famous Philosopher-Warrior-King of all of ancient Athens and arguably of all time, is known in history as "The Grand Uniter," much like Alexander the Great after him, but with much more swagger than swish. As I perused I saw other phrases I recognized too, many of which have long been burned into the Western psyche. Scalded might be a better term. For instance, "trust" was repeated a lot; "pride," too. "Mission accomplished" was not missed, nor was "family," and very especially "marriage," which even more frequently dotted the parchment pages. "Wanted, dead or alive," was on nearly every sheet, and "I am not a nation-builder" too, though nary once did I see it rephrased in the affirmative—"I am a nation destroyer"—for history shows that Bushistotle fostered progressive live-and-let-live policies as he and only he could define them: out with the bad guys and in with the good. Wherefore I was unsurprised to see "honesty" mentioned so often within this context of unbiased self-evaluation, and "compassionate" as well, and in the same vein—oh good fortune of good fortunes!—I happened upon the very page where lay the most famous quotation ever attributed to the Bushistotle Academy of Philosophy and Warfare, if not to Bushistotle himself—"Bring 'em on!"—a macho passage that almost always moves me to tears.

I was pretty much pooped after my long flight and cognac-laced meeting with Irma and Sister Naomi, so Irma tinkled another little bell and in marched Sister Mary Subjugation again to hustle me back to my cell, which is what "rooms" are called in the Vatican, and for good reason. I, on the other hand, eager to get this over with A.S.A.P. so I could do a little sightseeing, insisted on going immediately to the libary to start my project, but Mrs. Irma R. Gorgonzola nipped that right in the bud.

"Tomorrow," she said, "u a meet a dee a *cardinale*."

"Dee a *cardinale*?" I asked.

"*Sì. Cardinale Lei.*"

"The one who was smuggled under the cover of darkness out of the United States by the Vatican Swiss Guard?"

"*Sì*," Irma said. "He a inna charge a of a dee a Bushistotele project. Now u a go a to a u a cell. Nitey-nite!"

Mrs. Irma R. Gorgonzola waved her hand and Sister Mary Subjugation pushed me out of the office, and led me to my cell. Now you'd think that the Vatican would be just be bursting to the brim with nice rooms for people to stay in, but apparently the decorated ones are only for tourists, and since I was a de facto employee I got stuck in the staff quarters: five stone flights up, then down innumerable labyrinthine corridors one of which I was certain had to house a minotaur (or the pope), and we arrived at a plain wood-plank door with no knob just a rusty iron handle, that looked as if it had been snatched from the Hollywood set of Frankenstein. Sister Mary Subjugation took the crucifix that was dangling at her side, stuck it in the keyhole and unlocked the door with it, then she pushed both the door open and me inside. Then, just as quickly, she slammed it closed and locked it shut.

I was alone in the semidarkness and could hear Sister Mary Subjugation's footsteps echo down the hall as I felt my way around the room to see if I could find a light source. I was expecting the light to be a flame torch, and I imagined how difficult it would be to light without matches or a Bic, but eventually I stumbled upon what wound up being a cheap dime-store lamp with a 40-watt bulb, which vaguely illuminated my 6' x 6' cell: the room contained exactly one low and narrow bed that would better be described as a metal cot with an inch-thick straw mattress dressed with an airline pillow and blanket with "Alitalia" emblazoned across them (has the Vatican no shame?), and an old wooden table supporting a tastefully painted blue ceramic basin with a matching jug full of water and a plate of cheese and crackers. Barring the crucifix the walls were barren stucco, and barring nothing the floor was cold stone. No computer, no TV, no telephone, no board games, no cards, nothing! The window was 2' x 2' and covered with iron bars; I peeked out it, and not even a view! What had I journeyed all this way to Italy for if I didn't even have a room with a view?! Then—what's that over there?!—a BEDPAN! Not even a toilet but a BEDPAN! *How the hell do you use a BEDPAN?*

I thought, convinced that I wouldn't be able to crap for months. No wonder they call it a cell!

Then I saw my suitcase under the bed: it had been gone through and all my "reading material" had been removed; all I was left with was my underwear, toothbrush and toothpaste, and two meager changes of clothes, and a note addressed to me. I unfolded it, saw "You Are Being Held Incommunicado!" in bright red calligraphic writing. My first thought was no shit, Sherlock, I'm stuck in this goddamned cell, no phone, no television, no email, no toilet, nothing. Then underneath the "incommunicado" line I spied another, written in smaller handwriting, difficult to discern, which read: "You are in mortal danger! Comply for now, and eat this note lest it be found." As literature it was crappy and I thought it was a joke, so I tossed it in the bedpan.

The next morning, after having wolfed down the gorgonzola cheese and matzo crackers that had been left for me and washing them down with some of the nastiest tasting water ever—must've been Roman tap, cheapskates, not the French bottled shit I have a predilection for—and of course without having crapped, I awoke to a gentle knock on my door; when the door was opened (for I was locked inside) I was met by the initial gaggle of ironclad nuns who had escorted me to see Mrs. Irma R. Gorgonzola on my arrival. Leading them was Sister Naomi, who mumbled "achim sadoc abiud amon zorobabel" to me which, reflated back into English meant, "We're the Welcome Wagon, and we're here to welcome you onto our wagon!" With that, these black-robed dames with sensible shoes pulled me out of my cell, again pushed me and shoved me down the hall until I found myself once more standing in front of Mrs. Irma R. Gorgonzola's massive wooden door. So hard did these nuns push me that I scarcely had time to think about what they were welcome-wagoning me into, or onto, but that became clear as soon as the massive Mrs. Irma opened her mouth.

"Dank a u for a cumming," she said to me again, again with its double-entendre. "Back. I a hope a u a like a dee a cheese."

"I love gorgonzola," I told Mrs. Irma. R. Gorgonzola, buttering her up, so to speak.

"My a family, wee a bee a big a wigs a inna dee a cheese," she said. "Wee a give a dee a Vatican a big a discount. Dat's a how I gotta my a job."

I looked at her enormous girth. "Good for you!" I said. "More power to you! But could I have a better room, and my dirty magazines back?"

"Wee a see," Mrs. Irma R. Gorgonzola continued. "Itta depend onna u. U a see. Now, dee a *cardinale*, he a wanna meet a u."

Recalling the cardinal's torrid history in America, I said, "It's not really necessary, you know."

"Yes," Irma said. "He a want. Wee a go a now!"

Irma motioned the gaggle of ironclad nuns to hustle me into the cardinal's walnut-paneled suite, and in an instant I was there. Cardinal Lei, dapperly dressed in crimson with a matching crimson skullcap, polished wingtip shoes and designer socks, and definitely wearing trousers though I don't know about underwear under his cassock, was a tall, white-haired man. He extended his hand. "Nice to meet you, Steve."

The gaggle of nuns disappeared; I took Cardinal Lei's hand, then I sat. "Nice to meet you, too, Your Eminence." I lied.

"Just call me Bernie," the cardinal said.

"Thanks, Bernie."

"We're glad to have you on board, Steve!"

"Thank you, Bernie," I said. "Glad to lend my ancient Greek skills to anybody who needs them."

"I wanted to talk to you just to let you know how your valuable work fits into our project here at the Vatican. Background: for protecting the Church back home from quasi-scurrilous charges of sex abuse that I did my worldly best to keep secret, after my Rehabilitation I was clandestinely moved up the ranks and put in charge of the Department of Beatifications, Canonizations and Relics, which is responsible for making sure that we have a steady supply of candidates for sanctification. It's a P.R. thing."

"P.R.?"

"Right. P.R. That's what beatifications, canonizations and relics are all about—P.R. But I want more, Steve, and when I say I want more, I mean it. Beatifications, canonizations and relics are just one small part of the Vatican P.R. machine. We need the Division of Miracles under the same umbrella, but it's not. Some Italian running it, can't remember his name, a real fairy. The Church is full of them, and now that I've been rehabilitated I say it's time to fess up and out them all. Out them all on their fairy little asses. Never again will I take the fall for anybody, especially for those people. Turns my stomach, nearly botched my career."

"Right," I interjected. "Right."

"Anyhow, like I was saying," Bernie continued, "we need One Giant Umbrella, One Big Happy Family. We need the Publicity Department, we need the Marketing Department, we need the Direct Mail Department, we need the Parish Newsletter Department, we need the Monthly Missalettes Department, we need the New Psalms Department, we need the Sales Department and we need the Conversions Department all under one roof. Sales and Conversions are being merged into the Division of Proselytization, but that's a different story entirely. I supported the move for political purposes, but I don't like that word proselytization. Don't like that word...."

"I can understand," I sympathized.

"Basically, we need anything to do with communications to come under one roof, so the Church speaks with one voice."

"Yours?"

"It's a sacrifice, but I've been told by this pope that if I deliver real results, there's still a bright future for me in Rome."

"Where do I come in?"

"As part of a two-pronged effort," Bernie said. "My first job is the beatification of Bushistotle."

"The beatification of Bushistotle?"

"It's a pet project of this pope's, so there's no way out of it."

"St. Bushistotle?"

"Like I said, it's this pope's idea, and we have a 100-member task force working on it right now, scattered throughout the Vatican!"

"Scattered?"

"It's still Top Secret, but we're planning to go public once we get his two-plus miracles documented."

"I see. But Bushistotle was a pagan."

"Only by default, because Jesus wasn't born yet. Bushistotle was a very pious man, this pope says, and he led the very first crusade against the pagans."

"But he was a pagan himself! Not even Catholic!"

"But he would have been Catholic if he could have been, or so they say. I mean, the word here is that if Bushistotle were reborn today, all things being equal, he'd be reborn a Catholic. But honestly, between you and me—and keep this secret, please—I think it's the crusade thing. Somebody higher up's looking for a historical precedent for the First Crusade, declared by Pope Urban II in 1095. We're working on Urban II's canonization process right now under the code name Task Force U-2, but the whole declaring-war-for-no-apparent-reason thing is getting in the way, and that's where Bushistotle comes in. We name him a saint because of his crusade against the Persians, and bingo! U-2 can become a saint in the near future. It's called 'Rehabilitation,' which is probably why I'm in charge of it."

"How do you get around the fact that he wasn't Catholic?"

"Like I said, easy: because he couldn't have been. But obviously the Bushistotle Doctrine of Preemptive Retaliation was adopted by later Church officials, so there's relevancy there: both were dismal failures, and that's the perception we have to change. Remember, the Church is infallible, at least that's our claim, and historically it was Bushistotle's claim, too. So if we name Bushistotle a saint and he agrees with us in the historical record, a saint he must have been!"

"I guess...."

"Plus he already has one miracle to his name."

"Which was?"

"That anybody believed him."

"Doesn't he need two plus?"

"I'm in conversations with this pope right now: a miracle that big, I say, and you only need one. Plus it makes my job easier."

"Uhm...."

"Remember, Steve, I know what I'm talking about. We sowed the seeds for the beatification of Bushistotle years ago, in 1983, right after JP2 came in. One of the first things he did after getting rid of JP1 and purging the Curia of all its Second Vatican Council Leftist leftovers, was to change the rules for beatification, sort of like Roosevelt packing the Supreme Court. Used to be that you had to be dead 5 years before the process started, but that rule was laid out—ha! great the pun!—by U-7, Urban VII, in 1634. Well, tons has changed since then you gotta admit. First, people were named Urban back then, and you just don't see that a lot anymore. Then there were loads of saints back then, too, living among the people, and Jesus, Mary and Joseph *et al.* made phantasmagorical appearances on a regular basis to all sorts of illiterate peasants who would swear by it, but this stuff doesn't happen much anymore. So our thinking is that people are impatient for saints nowadays, the theory being that people want appearances."

"Appearances?"

"Appearances. People want appearances, just like in the olden days, so ergo, we had to speed the process up, and we did. This way people can say, 'I knew a saint! Imagine that, I knew a saint!' Or, 'Hey Ma, there's a saint on TV! There's a saint right there on the small screen!' Or, 'I saw a saint on an old newsreel!' Or, 'I saw a saint right after American Idol!' Or on the large screen or whatever, Steve, because the whole point is appearances, keeping up appearances! In the olden days it was phantasmagoria and statues, but nowadays live appearances is what makes the damn thing seem real! Celebrity is what makes the damn thing sell!"

"Celebrity?"

"How'd we do it, you ask? Good question! First, got rid of the prosecution, those nasty 'Devil's Advocates' people who dared to claim that one of our prescreened, preordained and preannointed candidates was unfit for sainthood. Who the hell do they think they are? I mean, really! That the Bushistotle Advance Team actually did long before the current campaign got started, to sow the seeds. To sow the seeds, that is, we instituted a Bushistotle Beatification Advance Team. We instituted an Advance Team to sow the seeds, which meant crushing the Devil's Advocates and anybody who'd challenge what we were saying about Bushistotle, our candidate, period, 'cause it's real bad press. Then for PXII—that's our code name for Pious XII—we lightened up the whole 'exemplary life' thing; it'll make it a lot easier for Pinochet once his turn comes up, too, which it will, right after Ferdinand and Isabella, and maybe Francisco Franco. Anyhow, those seemingly tiny changes will make it much easier for us to institute Summary Sainthood Proceedings, if you will, where you just say Wham! You're a saint! That's what we're heading towards: Wham! You're a saint!"

"Wham, you're a saint?"

"Exactly. In Italian they call it *santo subito*."

"*Santo subito?*"

That's right, and that's what we want. Look, this thing is totally doable: we did that Opus Dei creep's beatification in 5½ years, 11 years to sainthood: touchdown! Carlos Rodríguez took 9 years to score the winning goal and Pelé Zeferino Giménez Malla took 4, and who ever heard of them? Unless they're Colombian soccer players, nobody! Where's this leading, you ask? Good question. Toward Living Sainthood, that's where this is leading. You shorten the sainthood waiting list to a year, maybe two, then the question becomes why wait till somebody's dead, when they can't enjoy it, when you can name them a Living Saint right now? Think how inspiring that would be! Living Saints! Heroes, just like the kings of old! And of course appearances, appearances, appearances! Think of the cash flow from it. That was JP2's idea when he started all this back in '83, and I'm moving forward with it to its logical conclusion now."

"I see."

"I mean, you're a fan, too, Steve, so just think how much it would have helped Bushistotle's war against the Persians if the people in Bushistotle's time thought that he was a Living Saint, that everything he touched turned to gold if I might mix a metaphor or two! That's our goal, and hell, let's be honest: had I been alive back then with some of my marketing and P.R. ideas—Ready-Response teams and the like—all set to deflect any little bit of criticism that came his way, Bushistotle might have even won the whole goddamn war 'cause we would have convinced the goddamned Persians that they were going to lose! Hell, if I had been alive back then with my marketing and P.R. ideas, Christ might have even been born a few hundred years earlier, too, 'cause it would have been so much easier for Him to get His message out, without running such a high risk of crucifixion! God would have looked down from heaven in 350 BC, right when Bushistotle was living, and said to His only son, 'Jesus, why wait till Caesar? Just head on down right now, 'cause the world's got Bushistotle to contend with, and they need your message, big time.'"

"Really?"

"Absolutely! And I know this for a fact because I talked to this pope who told me that Jesus would've turned right back to God and said, 'Dad, you're right,' and like so many others He would have willingly died for the Bushistotle cause! And if that had happened then Bushistotle could've been a saint in the old-fashioned transfiguration slash loaves-and-fishes slash walk-on-water slash come-back-after-you-die sense, too, not just in this new sense that we're making up now, 'cause Jesus would've been right there to see to it that it got done! But Jesus wasn't there yet so Bushistotle was stuck in Limbo for like ever. You know, like 'Go to Limbo! Go Directly to Limbo! Do Not Pass Go! Do Not Collect $200!' That's what Limbo was back then, 'cause if you were born B.C. you just had to wait till Judgment Day when God would make up His mind in His own sweet time, and there were no guarantees and by definition no Christians to vouch for your good and honest nature. In other words your chances of Eternal Salvation were slim because there were no Chance, no Community Chest 'Get Out of Limbo Free' cards back then, for people born B.C., I mean."

"No."

"But remember, we solved that problem by getting rid of Limbo altogether, and between me and you we have the Bushistotle Advance Team to thank for that, too, because as long as he was in Limbo sainthood was out, and we would have had to wait till Judgment Day for Rehabilitation, which is way too late for our worldly purposes 'cause who knows when that will be? All earlier predictions were wrong so all bets are off. But the Advance Team saw that and took instant action years ago, removing one major obstacle to Bushistotle's candidacy for sainthood. So now it's up to me to take the next step—real live canonization, right after we get this slam-dunk beatification business out of the way!—and how we're going to do that is by removing the two other major obstacles that remain and make it look like a) his war against Persia was justified, and b) he did win it regardless of what the history books say. Then we can make him a real saint, which will in turn pave the way for the beatification of U-2 and who knows who else, maybe even Francisco Franco."

"Francisco Franco...?"

"Right. He's on the list, and believe me, this Bushistotle P.R. crusade will help. And it's totally doable, too. It's totally a faith-based initiative: we've done it before and we believe we can do it again!" Bernie winked at me. "Of course cleaning up Bushistotle's record won't be easy, but that's where you come in: spinning his pathetic history in a positive light to make him seem like a saint, that's our P.R. objective. It might kill you in the process—he-he-he!—but you'll get over it. Yes siree, Stevie-boy, you're going to make a fine new member of Task Force B.S.—that's our code name for Task Force Bushistotle—even if it kills you. But it's Top Secret—know what I mean?—so let's keep it mum." And he winked again.

Wham! You're a saint! rang through my head as I was being escorted back to Mrs. Irma R. Gorgonzola's office. *Wham! You're a saint!* But I didn't really want Bushistotle to become a saint. It was bad enough that he was known as "History's Greatest Philosopher-Warrior-King," but "History's Greatest Saint-Philosopher-Warrior-King" was more than I could stomach, especially if any of my translation work were used to support his candidacy.

On my return I found Mrs. Gorgonzola still in a good mood, and again we shared a couple or more (or even more) chalicefuls of brandy—seems she was as a big a fan of the stuff as I was: must be a Catholic laypeople thing—and some more gorgonzola cheese on matzo. Yum, but after my meeting with Cardinal Bernie I needed a lot to drink: not being big on crusades or global conquest, distorting the record of Bushistotle's rule to make it all seem like a good idea wasn't something I thought I was capable of doing; I thought his record spoke for itself. But in the end I decided that since I was there I'd make the best of it, because the alcohol seemed to flow freely: two brandies after dizziness had set in I knew I'd had almost enough to drink, and was nearly ready for work. I ordered one more for the road, but before I departed Mrs. Irma R. Gorgonzola summarily informed me of the rules. "O a kay," she said. "U a can a go a to a dee libary, but first a, dee a rules."

"Rules?" I inquired.

"Yes a, dee a rules," she answered. "U a heedins, u a not allowed to a circulate a freely in a dee a Vatican."

"Heedins?" I inquired.

"Yes a, heedins," she answered.

"What's a 'heedin?'" I inquired.

"A heedin is a peeples who donna believe in a God."

"Heedins donna believe inna God?" I further inquired.

"Dats a right."

Perplexed at the meaning of this, I thought a moment: *Heedins donna believe inna God. Heedins donna believe inna God. Heedins donna believe inna God.* Then Sister Naomi briefly stopped her Lemon Pledging—she had by now moved on to the dusty oversized St.-Francis-of-Assisi-holding-a-vicious-looking-squirrel-in-his-arms statue that was pleasantly tucked away in a distant corner—shuffled over and whispered "achim sadoc abiud amon zorobabel" into my ear again, and I got it: <u>Heathens</u> don't believe in God. <u>Heathens</u> are not allowed to circulate freely in the Vatican! <u>Heathens</u>! Ha! I was a <u>Heathen</u>!

How dare she!

Indignant, I thought for yet another moment, tried to come up with an objection to her classification of me as godless, but in the end I knew I would have to concur: I am indeed a heathen.

"But how do you know I'm a heedin?" I asked her, just for sport.

"Wee a do our a *investigazioni*," she said.

"Fair enough. But the ancients were a heedins, as well."

"Dats a right," Irma shot back. "Dee a ancients was a heedins as a well. So a dats dee a second part of a dee a rules: wee a can't allow a dis a book out of our a *visione*, dat is a, out of our a sight, so a u a gonna have a—how a u say?—*un angelo custode*."

"Guardian angel," I answered, summoning up my best Italian.

"Dats a right." Irma said.

"Dats a right?"

"Dats a right," Irma said. "*Avrai un angelo custode*." Then she pointed straight at my guardian angel: Sister Mary Subjugation. I would have preferred a young priest, but young priests prefer young boys, so I guess it would have to work out for the best between me and Sister Mary S. "And a dee a book a," Mrs. Irma R. Gorgonzola continued, "u a canna not a read a it *senza di lei*."

"What?" I asked, my Italian virtually exhausted.

"U a can use a dee book only when a dee sister she be a wit a u. Deeze a heedin books, dey a can a contain a bad a ideas a dat a wee a have a to a get a rid a of, so His a Holiness, dee a *papa*, he a have a to a read u a translation before anybody else, and a dat be a dee a job of a dee sister, to a make a sure."

Clear enough, so after bidding ado to Mrs. Irma R. Gorgonzola and Sister Naomi, Sister Mary Subjugation and I were off; soon we arrived at the Vatican Secret Archives, and what a fancy-schmancy place it is! Paintings all over the ceiling that made my once-fashionable popcorn one back home look like absolute shit; I made a mental note to buy a package of naked-people stencils with my earnings once I returned stateside, to see if I could duplicate the effect, liven my desolate apartment up. One thing's for sure: maybe they are lousy soldiers, but Italians sure do have the one-up on us when it comes to interior decorating!

I had expected the Vatican Secret Archives to be full of myopic monks dressed in brown horsehair robes tied together with frayed rope, wearing smelly sandals that looked like they'd walked to Jerusalem and back by themselves, stuffed till they overflowed with fat feet clad in standard-issue white socks bereft of elastic and falling to their ankles, all of said so-dressed monks dutifully copying illuminated manuscripts by candlelight, slowly going blind. But boy was I surprised! It was actually a modern, albeit well-funded, libary, with computer terminals and everything, inhabited by scholars and other sundry oddballs interested in trying to figure out exactly what had gone wrong over the centuries with the Church of Rome—had they asked me I could have volunteered some of my own personal theories, but they didn't—plus a few priests who I would later find were secretaries and the like to the Curia, busy doing research for the next set of rules to be issued by the pope that nobody in the world would pay attention to at all, anyway. Sometimes you wonder why he bothers.

Yet there was something eerie about this place: as soon as I entered, all eyes turned my way, whisked as I was through the main reading room and into a barren, soundproof side room with a fishbowl window that contained one computer terminal, two exceedingly uncomfortable-looking straight-backed wooden chairs, and one study carrel: the Isolation Booth! The only decoration beyond the omnipresent crucifix was a forlorn sign on the wall that read *Divieto di Usare Telefonini*: "Cell Phone Use Prohibited."

I had left my cell phone back in America, which a) made me the only person in Italy without one, and b) made the sign moot. Sister Mary Subjugation plopped the text on the desktop of the study carrel, then indicated with her long and crooked index finger that I was to sit in the exceedingly uncomfortable-looking straight-backed wooden chair behind it. Then she sat in the exceedingly uncomfortable-looking straight-backed wooden chair next to mine, and glared, and pointed for me to start work.

Since I really didn't know much ancient Greek (or any at all) I ripped out my handy pocket dictionary, spent the next several hours picking through its dog-eared pages translating, translating, translating, as Sister Mary Subjugation peered over my shoulder. It was worth the effort, however, because the picture that eventually emerged was amazing:

Proud Bushistotle, the legendary Philosopher-Warrior-King of Athens and Headmaster of the Athens Academy of Philosophy and Warfare, dressed in his finest white toga, was lounging amongst his followers in the Academy's Sacred House, sometimes called the Bushistotle Center, nestled quaintly in the suburbs of Athens, surrounded by olive trees and a heavy stone wall. The mid-September afternoon was sunny and a light breeze blew; lunch had just been served, and the Bushistotle Coterie was just passing the time: tee-off was scheduled for four.

"Great lunch!" Bushistotle said to the waiter. "What was it?"

"Gyros," answered the waiter.

"Delicious," said Bushistotle.

Powellonius raised his cup: "Hail Honorable Bushistotle!"

He was seconded by Constantina, who also raised her cup: "Indeed!"

The rest of the Coterie present—Ashcroftus, Cheneyon—raised their cups as well, and all shouted, "Hail Honorable Bushistotle!" *All, that is, but the wait staff, who were contemplating a strike to raise their salaries just a notch above the minimum wage.*

Overcome with gratitude, Bushistotle ignored the help and raised his cup to salute his comrades-in-arms: "Well hail right back to you, Honorable Guys!" *cried Bushistotle, seemingly overcome with emotion. He paused a moment to compose himself.* "Okay, now that our stomachs are full and our heads a little dizzy from those frozen whatevers—at least mine is: been meaning to swear off that stuff—time for business. Sometimes it's important to state the obvious, and I'm pretty darn good at it which is why I'm in charge, so here goes: Athens is a great republic...."

"But you said you were going to read us an after-dinner story!" protested Constantina.

"Yes, a story," said Ashcroftus. "Before golf."

"I did, didn't I?" responded Bushistotle. *He lifted the book that was on the floor next to where he lounged.* "I'm going to read more of Mrs. Bushistotle's new work about our pet donkey on the ranch!"

"Oh great!" cried Cheneyon.

"I love Mrs. Bushistotle's stories," said Ashcroftus.

"Me too," added Constantina.

"Yes, me, too," said Bushistotle. "She has so much literary style! Now then, to begin my lovely wife's story, <u>Dudley the Donkey Learns a Lesson</u>: 'Dudley was a wonderful gray donkey who lived on the Bushistotle family *farm in the Macedonian Outback, but Dudley loved to eat the leftovers from the Bushistotles' garbage. One day Mrs. Bushistotle said to her husband Bushistotle, the Philosopher-Warrior-King of Athens:* "Please don't let the donkey eat the leftovers in our garbage, my darling Bushistotle, the Philosopher-Warrior-King of Athens. "The neighbors will think we don't feed him!"

""'Yes," said Bushistotle, the Philosopher-Warrior-King of Athens, to Mrs. Bushistotle, "you are correct. We must train Dudley the Donkey to eat donkey food, just like babies eat baby food!"

""'You are so smart and loving," Mrs. Bushistotle said to Bushistotle, the Philosopher-Warrior-King of Athens. "Now I know why I married you!""

Suddenly, the only missing member of the Coterie, Rumsfeldiavelli, who had been jogging laps in the nearby Gymnasium, burst into the Sacred House. "Spartan terrorists have attacked the Athenian colony at Syracuse!" he announced.

Bushistotle had no reaction; he just sat there for a moment.

"Spartan terrorists have attacked the Athenian colony at Syracuse!" Rumsfeldiavelli repeated.

Bushistotle looked confused; he just sat there for a moment.

"Spartan terrorists have attacked the Athenian colony at Syracuse!" Rumsfeldiavelli repeated again.

"The Athenian colony where?" Bushistotle finally asked.

"At Syracuse!"

"We have a colony in New York?" Bushistotle asked. "We don't even like New York."

"No," Rumsfeldiavelli answered. "I mean yes, but no. Not Syracuse, New York. Syracuse, Sicily."

"Oh," Bushistotle answered. "We have a colony in Sicily?"

"Yes," answered Powellonius. "Athens has colonies everywhere, and you visited it last year."

Bushistotle resumed reading his donkey story aloud.

"But aren't we going to do anything?" interrupted Ashcroftus. "Arrest anyone?"

"Yes!" cried Constantina. "We need to take action!"

"But don't you want to hear the story that Mrs. Bushistotle wrote about our pet donkey?" Bushistotle asked. "Don't you want to know how it ends?"

"You need to make a decision!" Rumsfeldiavelli cried. "A decision!"

"Oh," said Bushistotle. "A decision. Well, if Spartan terrorists have attacked us in Sicily, we must declare war on Persia!"

"Why?" asked Powellonius. "That makes absolutely no sense!"

"Hear, hear!" said Constantina. "They are part of the Axis of Evil!"

"War on Persia!" Rumsfeldiavelli cried. "War on Persia!"

"Because your enemy's enemy is your enemy," Bushistotle answered. "The old outage...."

"Adage," Powellonius corrected. "Adage."

"Can I please finish reading Mrs. Bushistotle's story?" Bushistotle complained. "There are still a lot of important lessons for Dudley the Donkey to learn!"

Right here Sister Mary Subjugation slapped me on the wrist, indicated to me that I should give the keyboard to her, which I did. She looked over what I had written, shook her head no, then began to edit it. First she added text to my translation, which text was not at all in the original: *"Spartan terrorists, aided and abetted by Persia, have attacked the Athenian colony at Syracuse!" he announced.*

Well, I thought, *that sure does make the war sound more justifiable*.

After a pause for more review Sister Mary Subjugation began to delete some of the original text by rather violently striking the backspace key, and all of a sudden this was gone: *{Bushistotle had no reaction; he just sat there for a moment}*.

Yikes! A major part of the story had just been obliterated by a nun!

But she wasn't done, as nuns on a roll never seem to be. She obliterated more and more of my text: *{"Spartan terrorists have attacked the Athenian colony at Syracuse!" Rumsfeldiavelli repeated.}*

"Hey!" I shouted.

She deleted: *{Bushistotle looked confused; he just sat there for a moment.}*

"Hey! I like that!"

More deletions: *{"Spartan terrorists have attacked the Athenian colony at Syracuse!" Rumsfeldiavelli repeated again.}*

"Put that back!"

But she just kept on deleting: *{"The Athenian colony where?" Bushistotle finally asked.}*

{"At Syracuse!"}

{"We have a colony in New York?" Bushistotle asked. "We don't even like New York."}

{"No," Rumsfeldiavelli answered. "I mean yes, but no. Not Syracuse, New York. Syracuse, Sicily."}

{"Oh," Bushistotle answered. "We have a colony in Sicily?"}

{"Yes," answered Powellonius. "Athens has colonies everywhere, and you visited it last year."}

{Bushistotle resumed reading his donkey story aloud.}

{"But aren't we going to do anything?" asked Ashcroftus. "Arrest anyone?"}

{"Yes!" cried Constantina. "We need to take action!"}

{"But don't you want to hear the story that Mrs. Bushistotle wrote about our pet donkey?" Bushistotle asked. "Don't you want to know how it ends?"}

{"You need to make a decision!" Rumsfeldiavelli cried. "A decision!"}

Sister Mary Subjugation clicked on the "Save" icon, and I couldn't believe my eyes: a lowly nun had just changed history! I confronted her: "But Sister Mary Subj...." Then I remembered that I didn't actually know her nun-name and had made "Sister Mary Subjugation" up. Since she might not be as enamored of it as I was, I started over again, this time more tactfully: "But Sister, how can you just change history like that, with just a stroke of the keyboard?"

Always perfectly in character, Sister Mary Subjugation said nothing.

"Is it to paint Bushistotle in a better light?" I asked, without revealing too much of what I knew of Cardinal Bernie's Top Secret Task Force B.S. Project for fear of the Inquisition, though I suspected that Sister Mary Subjugation could be part of it, too.

Sister Mary Subjugation said nothing.

"Is it pro-Bushistotle spin, to make him seem smart?"

Sister Mary Subjugation again said nothing; rather, she just went right on editing, striking out: {"*Oh,*" *said Bushistotle. "A decision. Well,*}. Then she let the story run a bit, keeping "*if Spartan terrorists have attacked us in Sicily....*" Then she began to add text: "*...aided and abetted by Persia," Bushistotle said, "we must also declare war on Persia since we are already at war with Sparta!*"

The end result was that the true story, which originally read, "*Well, if Spartan terrorists have attacked us in Sicily, we must declare war on Persia!*" had now been edited by a minion at the Catholic Church to read: "*Well, if Spartan terrorists have attacked us in Sicily, aided and abetted by Persia, we must also declare war on Persia since we are already at war with Sparta!*"

"But Sister!" I cried. "That's not true!"

Undeterred, Sister Mary Subjugation continued to delete: *{"Why?" asked Powellonius. "That makes absolutely no sense!"}* Then, however, she let the true story run, because the "Axis of Evil" business suited her nefariously orthodox purpose: "*Hear, hear!" said Constantina. "They are part of the Axis of Evil!*"

"*War on Persia!" Rumsfeldiavelli cried. "War on Persia!*"

Then she deleted, probably as unbecoming: *{"Because your enemy's enemy is your enemy," Bushistotle answered. "The old outage...."}*

Deleted: *{"Adage," Powellonius corrected. "Adage."}*

Deleted: *{"Can I please finish reading Mrs. Bushistotle's story?" Bushistotle complained.}*

Added: <u>"*We are not rushing to war," said Bushistotle, "but they have asked for it!*"</u>

"But you're changing history, Sister!" I protested yet again.

And though she seemed not to care, she had changed history, because my original story about Bushistotle was now entirely different, making him seem like someone he was not. Now it read: *Suddenly, the only missing member of the Coterie, Rumsfeldiavelli, who had been jogging laps in the nearby Gymnasium, burst into the Sacred House. "Spartan terrorists, aided and abetted by Persia, have attacked the Athenian colony at Syracuse!" he announced.*

"*If Spartan terrorists have attacked us in Sicily, aided and abetted by Persia,*" *Bushistotle said, "we must also declare war on Persia since we are already at war with Sparta!*"

"*War on Persia!" Rumsfeldiavelli cried. "War on Persia!*"

"*Hear, hear!" said Constantina. "They are part of the Axis of Evil!*"

"*We are not rushing to war," said Bushistotle, "but they have asked for it!*"

"But Sister," I protested again. "We can't publish this! This is not what Bushistotle is known to have said or done! Bushistotle declared war for no reason! Like Bushistotle's own people, you have spun this story into something that it is not!"

And that was true, but between me and you and since Sister Mary Subjugation sadly is no longer in the picture, I have to be honest and say that despite my protestations I'm not exactly one hundred percent sure that what I had translated and what Sister Mary Subjugation was changing were the exact words that appeared on the exact piece of parchment I was translating since a) I was kind of tired after such a long trip and so many thirst-quenching cognacs, and b) I don't speak ancient Greek, despite my website claims. Nonetheless I think I got the "feeling" of what was said, which is what's important. That is, even if it wasn't the word-for-word truth, I think that it's what the original should have said had the author known what we all know today about Bushistotle: hindsight is 20-20, and history is written from the point-of-view of the winner, and in this case I'm the winner.

But Sister Mary Subjugation paid no attention to my complaints; rather she made typing gestures in the air, which I took as my signal to get back to work, which I did, of course under her ever-watchful eye: *""But how do you go about training a donkey?" Mrs. Bushistotle asked Bushistotle, the Philosopher-Warrior-King of Athens.*

""Well," answered Bushistotle, the Philosopher-Warrior-King of Athens, "I think the key is to teach the donkey right from wrong."

""As you have taught the Athenian people right from wrong?" Mrs. Bushistotle asked.

""Yes," answered Bushistotle, the Philosopher-Warrior-King of Athens.

""But how do you do that?" asked Mrs. Bushistotle.

""Why of course by teaching him the difference between good and bad!" answered Bushistotle, the Philosopher-Warrior-King of Athens.""

As Bushistotle was busy reading his wife's story to the Coterie, Rumsfeldiavelli began to grow anxious and pace about the Sacred House, up and down its central corridor. But knowing that Bushistotle liked to finish one thought before moving slowly on to the next, Rumsfeldiavelli held his peace. The other members of the Coterie began to fidget, as well, sensing that something needed to be done quickly about Sparta's attack on Syracuse lest a vital opportunity be lost, but they, too, held their peace as Bushistotle continued reading.

""What is the difference between good and bad?" asked Mrs. Bushistotle.

""Why, it's obvious," said Bushistotle, the Philosopher-Warrior-King of Athens.

""I see," said Mrs. Bushistotle. "So we have to teach Dudley the Donkey the obvious?"

""""Yes," answered Bushistotle, the Philosopher-Warrior-King of Athens. "And who better to teach Dudley the obvious than me?"

"And with that Bushistotle, the Philosopher-Warrior-King of Athens, set out to teach Dudley the Donkey all the things that seemed obvious to him. He sat Dudley the Donkey down on a bench on the back porch of the Big House at his ranch in the Macedonian Outback, had Mrs. Bushistotle sit right next to Dudley, and he began to explain the difference between good and bad.

""""The first thing you need to be good," explained Bushistotle, the Philosopher-Warrior-King of Athens, to Dudley the Donkey and to Mrs. Bushistotle, "is to be a uniter, because families are better united."

""""You mean because the family that prays together stays together?" Mrs. Bushistotle interjected.

""""Exactly, my lovely Mrs. Bushistotle," said Bushistotle, the Philosopher-Warrior-King of Athens. "It's God's plan. So if it is good to be a uniter, what is it bad to be?" Bushistotle, the Philosopher-Warrior-King of Athens, looked expectantly at his pupils, but no one volunteered an answer. "Dudley?" said Bushistotle, the Philosopher-Warrior-King of Athens, to Dudley the Donkey. "Any ideas?"

"But Dudley the Donkey didn't answer.

""""I'm disappointed with you for not having an answer," said Bushistotle, the Philosopher-Warrior-King of Athens, to Dudley the Donkey. "I was hoping for more!"

"Dudley the Donkey brayed sadly.

""""But that's okay," said Bushistotle, the Philosopher-Warrior-King of Athens. "It happens to me, too, sometimes, and when I don't know the answer to something I always turn to Mrs. Bushistotle. So, does Mrs. Bushistotle know what it's bad to be if it's good to be a uniter?"

"Mrs. Bushistotle raised her hand. "Oh, I know! I know!"

""""Yes, Mrs. Bushistotle?" said Bushistotle, the Philosopher-Warrior-King of Athens, calling on Mrs. Bushistotle. "What's it bad to be if it's good to be a uniter?"

""""It's bad to be a divider," answered Mrs. Bushistotle, "if it's good to be a uniter!"

""""That's right!" said Bushistotle, the Philosopher-Warrior-King of Athens. "Good for you! It's bad to be a divider if it's good to be a uniter. Therefore, if it's good to be a uniter then it's right to be a uniter, and if it's bad to be a divider then it's wrong to be a divider. In my philosophy it is called the unity of opposites, which is God's plan, and it forms the basis of my nonpartisan rule of Athens!"

"With that, and finally feeling like a full member of the all-inclusive Bushistotle family, Dudley the Donkey brayed in happiness...."

Right at this critical juncture in my translation—with Bushistotle explaining his philosophy of governance to Mrs. Bushistotle and Dudley the Donkey, with Rumsfeldiavelli pacing the central corridor of the Sacred House, and with the rest of the Bushistotle Coterie fidgeting expectantly in hopes that Bushistotle would make a decision on what to do about Sparta's attack on Athens' colony in Sicily besides nonsensically declaring war on Persia in retaliation—I hit a giant snag: my first major Windex blotch that obscured the original text!

I was of three minds about this Windex blotch: first, I was absolutely furious at Sister Naomi for not knowing that ancient ink runs. Second, I was glad that it would give me the opportunity to exegete a bit on the text—that is, to make stuff up—since like me, nobody else could figure out what the original text said, anyway. And third, I was elated that I finally had an excuse to stop translating awhile, because my eyes were killing me.

I looked over my shoulder at Sister Mary Subjugation: her ever-watchful eyes were closed, and she was soundly sleeping. Or, perhaps more appropriately in her case, recharging: Matins must be too early in the morning for her very evil, I mean very fragile, constitution.

Now stoic isn't the kindest of monikers you can attach to a fellow human being, but it seemed if anything an understatement in Sister Mary Subjugation's case. Overall I would say that even when sleeping she looked closest to the evil Emperor in <u>Star Wars</u>, though his posture was straighter, he had a few dozen fewer wrinkles, and a much better sense of humor. Whenever during my stay at the Vatican I saw her I fully expected Sister Mary Subjugation to extend her arms and zap me with some form of high-intensity alien energy that would spew from her fingernails, yet throughout our many months together she never actually did.

I thought I might nudge her to wake her up, but then I changed my mind: the worst thing to do to anybody who harbors alien energy forms in their fingernails is to startle them, else they might instinctively zap you in their somnolescence. In Sister Mary Subjugation's case, it would be akin to tapping a porcupine on the shoulder and asking him to get out of your driveway; best wait till he wakes up in his own good time.

Then I realized that her nascent narcolepsy also gave me an unparalleled opportunity to set the record straight, document for all posterity what I thought the legendary Bushistotle, the Philosopher-Warrior-King of Athens, had said (whether he had actually said it or not), and not what Sister Mary Subjugation wanted him to have said (whether he had actually said it or not), by undoing the changes that Sister Mary Subjugation had made to my translation.

This meant that I was faced with a dilemma faced by so many Catholics before, during, and after me: whether I should do what I thought was right, or whether I should do what the Church—qua Sister Mary Subjugation and Cardinal Bernie Lei—thought was right, when it was plain that neither of us was absolutely right, and both of us, in fact, were mostly wrong. I tried to think the problem through within the context of Dudley the Donkey—which action would be good, and therefore right?—and after about a minute of internal debate I vowed never to err on the side of somebody else's righteousness again.

With this thought I felt a pang of guilt simultaneous with a rush of exhilaration, like a college freshman who has finally figured out that you don't actually have to show up for class since the professor doesn't take attendance, and who decides to give hooky a shot. So, since Sister Mary Subjugation was still sound asleep, I set to work immediately by changing her inaccurate changes to the original text right back to my original inaccurate translation of it. Maybe it's a genetic thing, but if anybody was going to leave his mark on the "true" history of Bushistotle, the legendary Philosopher-Warrior-King of Athens, I'd rather it be me than the Vatican, because I have a better sense of humor!

I started with her correction, *"Spartan terrorists, aided and abetted by Persia, have attacked the Athenian colony at Syracuse!"* and changed it back to, *"Spartan terrorists have attacked the Athenian colony at Syracuse."* Then I added back the deleted lines starting from, *"Bushistotle had no reaction; he just sat there for a moment"* through *"'You need to make a decision!' Rumsfeldiavelli cried. 'A decision!'"* Then I turned *"'If Spartan terrorists have attacked us in Sicily, aided and abetted by Persia,' Bushistotle said, 'we must also declare war on Persia since we are already at war with Sparta!'"* back into *"'Oh,' said Bushistotle. 'A decision. Well, if Spartan terrorists have attacked us in Sicily, we must declare war on Persia!'"*

Sister Mary Subjugation must have heard the delete key or

something, because she shot up ramrod straight; were I a pop-psychologist I would speculate that her nap had taken her somewhat by surprise, and by unpleasant surprise, at that. Compassionate myself by nature, if Sister Mary S. were more open to interaction I would have told her not to worry because I used to fall asleep in philosophy class all the time, too, but I decided not to get too chummy lest she misread it; best to let her make the first move on the friendship front, I thought.

After using her long and crooked fingernail to extract copious amounts of sand from her eyes—she must have had an untreated sinus ailment—Sister Mary Subjugation flicked a last bit of mucous my way (though without spewing any of that pent-up alien energy I just knew she had stored in her fingernails), thereby unclogging her laser fingernail as if she were a cobra cleaning its fangs. With her nail newly cleaned she hit "undo" "undo "undo" a number of times in a row until the text that I had changed had been restored back to her version of it, then she erased the entire—and endearing—Dudley the Donkey story I had translated while she was asleep.

She slammed the book closed, clutched it to her breast. Normally, of course—gentleman that I am—I would have offered to carry such a heavy burden for a lady, but instinct told me that approaching a nun's bosom, even to offer her aid (and especially to offer her succor), might not be the wisest of diplomatic moves: the Vatican Swiss Guard, all dandily dressed up donning duds designed by none other than Michelangelo himself, may not look all too menacing to, say, the U.S. Army, but they do brandish long and pointy spears.

Sister Mary Subjugation grabbed me by the ear, yanked me out of the Isolation Booth and through the Vatican's Secret Archives. "Ooouch! Ooouch!" I cried through the Archives. "But I can't conform! I can't conform! I can't write good things about Bushistotle! He's not a saint! Lies! I can't! Lies!" I screamed more and more, and all eyes were upon me, but because I was being dragged my head was tilted to one side, which allowed me to see, yonder, under an Italian sign that more or less equated to "Reference Desk" in English, what I had been expecting: a myopic monk dressed in brown horsehair robes tied together with frayed rope, wearing sandals that looked like they'd walked to Jerusalem and back by themselves, stuffed till they overflowed with fat feet clad in standard-issue white socks bereft of elastic and falling to his ankles. I decided I would call him Fra Diavolo.

That night I felt the full power of the Roman Inquisition: they sent me to bed without supper! I was merely dragged by the ear into my cell and locked in, and all that had been left for me was yet another pitcher of stale Roman tap water—yuck!—and a handful of matzo crumbs. Ominously, a new message had been left for me: "You Are Being Held Prisoner!"

Oh, please, stop with the notes! I thought, and tossed this one into the bedpan, as well. I lay down on my cot, pulled the Alitalia blanket over me and and tried to get somewhat comfortable, but then I started thinking: would they really let me die if I refused to comply with their demand to alter history as I had invented it? At first I thought not, but then the words of Mrs. Irma R. Gorgonzola's original email to me flooded my mind: "Wee a unnerstand a dat a u is a—how a u a say a, *'traduttore?'*—of a ancient Greek a, and a all a of a our a ancient Greeks a here a is a dead."

All of their ancient Greeks is a dead! I had thought she meant that it was because all ancient Greeks is a dead, period, and that's what I had originally taken that sentence to mean, and why I figured it was a joke. Now, however, its sinister meaning was being revealed. But how could I allow myself to be forced into making Bushistotle into what I knew him not to be? Sister Mary Subjugation wanted him decisive whereas I saw a moron, and I was obviously right and she was obviously wrong. Then it came crashing down upon me that unless I complied I could remain locked in my cell and held as a prisoner of war; I wondered whether the Geneva Conventions would apply.

Hypoglycemia and exhaustion play strange tricks on the mind, and as I lay on the cot I drifted between consciousness and un-. I was in a state wherein I knew I could not trust my senses, but wherein I could not control what I sensed, either. In other words, I was in a middling state, like stoned, man, and in such a state I saw myself held prisoner in a cage on the Macedonian Outback, with Dudley the Donkey and Bushistotle sitting on a bench on the back porch of his ranch in judgment of me, and Mrs. Bushistotle, donning a frilly gingham apron, nonchalantly baking a shoofly pie inside, as Ashcroftus—or was it Rumsfeldiavelli, or Constantina, or some other shadowy figure?—acting as prosecutor, explained to them why the Geneva Conventions do not apply to me and other recent prisoners of war.

"As I have said," this shadowy figure began, "the Culture War is a new kind of war. It is not the traditional clash between nations adhering to the law, but rather one of activist judges inventing the law, and of left-wing subversives subverting it. Therefore the nature of the Culture War places a high premium on special factors, such as conformism, the ability to quickly spin current events, and to distort the truth to make it fit our paradigm. So by concluding that the Geneva Conventions do not apply to prisoners of the Culture War, we hold open options for future cultural conflicts, allowing us to determine what actions we can take against Enemy Combatants—'Cultural Terrorists,' if you will—because that we must take action, and fast action, in order to prevail, is not in dispute."

"Hear, hear!" shouted Bushistotle, but Dudley the Donkey looked over at me and brayed helplessly in sadness. I, on the other hand, appear to have sat silent in my cage.

The shadowy figure continued: "Some of the language in the Geneva Conventions is undefined. What, for example, is an 'outrage upon personal dignity' and 'inhuman treatment,' except what it is to the beholder? Thus we are justified in holding prisoners of the Culture War in preventive detention without specific charges, for what charges could be levied but treason, which is a real bear to prove even though we know it's true? Recall that the Conventions require that severe pain and suffering 'be inflicted with specific intent' but though it could be construed by some as an 'outrage upon personal dignity' or an instance of 'inhuman treatment,' sending a prisoner of the Culture War to bed without supper is not specifically intended to cause pain and suffering, though that may be the end result of it. It is not torture but rather persuasion, whose specific intent is to get such prisoner to conform to the way that history as we have written it shows that the world has always been, and to convince his friends to do the same. What is wrong with that?"

"Guilty!" shouted Bushistotle. "Guilty!"

"Hang him!" cried Mrs. Bushistotle from the kitchen, dipping her finger into the shoofly pie. "Hang him!"

"Braaaaaaay!" brayed Dudley the Donkey in vehement objection. "Braaaaaaay!"

The jury was back and 2-to-1, I had been convicted! Dudley the

Donkey brayed "braaaaaaaay" again in my ears as I felt my cage being dragged away so I could be further tortured by Bushistotle. I awoke a bit from my semi-dream state on account of the braying in my head, looked up at the wall-mounted crucifix, wondered whether I could use it as a key to open my cell, much as Sister Mary Subjugation had used the crucifix on the end of the rosary strung around her waste to open it. I looked at the keyhole and I looked at the cross, and I realized that the cross was too big and would not unlock my door. *Some crosses must be more equal than others*, I thought, and I now felt how Sister Mary Subjugation must have felt: take away a person's ability to communicate and you do not change who he is; you only take away his humanity. No wonder the bitch was such a bitch!

How much torture would be necessary for me to give in to the Vatican and write about the legendary Bushistotle, the Philosopher-Warrior-King of Athens, what they wanted me to write about him rather than what I knew to be true or—better—what I wanted to to be true? I was starving now, but how much hungrier would I have to grow before I would acquiesce to their demands? Would I be forced to attend Mass just to get something to eat? And even if I did acquiesce to the Church's demands would they ever release me to the outside world? I thought not, for if they did I would be free to tell the world of the torture I had endured under the cruel reign of the Catholic Church, and how they had tried to make me conform against my will.

As I lay on my cot I grew ever more certain that the Vatican would never let me go even if I did conform to what they wanted me to do, even if I did cause Bushistotle's behavior to conform to what they wanted him to have done by falsifying my already sort-of-invented translation. I dozed off trying to plan ways to escape, but given the circumstances and the nunly *angelo custode* at my side at all times it seemed an unlikely proposition.

There was a knock on the door; I shot up. The door swung wide open: it was morning, just post-Matins, I assumed, and I was looking right at Sister Mary Subjugation again. How delightful! This time, though, she held a small piece of paper and some Scotch tape; she taped a sign onto the wall—*Divieto di Usare Telefonini*—right under the crucifix, and motioned for me to follow her.

No breakfast: I brushed my teeth and put on clothes (with Sister Mary Subjugation watching: yuck!), then she tugged me by my ear the what-seemed-to-be-several-miles back to Mrs. Irma R. Gorgonzola's office. I'm not quite sure what it is, but there's something archetypal about walking down a hallway being dragged by the ear by a nun: you get this overwhelming feeling that you've done something wrong. You feel wracked by guilt and shame, and every time someone passes you by you just know that they're looking at you like you're about to be hauled in front of the principal, and will be forced to recite the rosary one thousand times aloud and then get your ass kicked by your classmates for forcing them to sit through it, or you'll be forced to write out the Act of Contrition longhand until, stigmata-like, your fingertips start to bleed.

We found Mrs. Gorgonzola in her office, eating an early morning platter of spaghetti as she waited for us. "Good a day," Mrs. Irma R. Gorgonzola said, addressing me. "U a done a berry good a job."

"What?"

Irma picked a dot-matrix printout up from her desk that she had been using as a placemat, and handed it to me. I looked it over; it contained the first text that I had translated—*"Spartan terrorists have attacked the Athenian colony a Syracuse!" he announced*—but in the version edited by Sister Mary Subjugation: *"Spartan terrorists, **aided and abetted by Persia**, have attacked the Athenian colony at Syracuse!" he announced.*

"Dis a bee a berry good a translation," Irma said. "True a to a dee a history. But den a," Irma continued, "you a did a—how a u say?—a no-a-no."

"A no-a-no?"

"A no-a-no."

"What did I do?"

Mrs. Irma R. Gorgonzola ripped a sheet off the dot-matrix printer, handed it to me. It contained the full history of all the text I had typed into the word processor, and every change made to it.

"Wee a keep a dee a different *versioni* dat a u a write," Irma R. Gorgonzola said. "And a wee a see dat a u a change a dee Sister's a redacted a text a. Dat a no-a-no!"

"But Mrs. Gorgonzola," I pleaded, "Sister Mary Subj..., I mean the good Sister here changed the text of my translation!"

"And whatta u a point?"

"My point is that what she has written doesn't say what the

original says! It's not what the true history of Bushistotle is! It's just another bunch of lies!"

"Yes a," said Mrs. Irma R. Gorgonzola. "Itta not what dee a *originale* say, but even iffa itta not a dee a word-a-for-a-word trut, eye a tink a dat a it's a whatta dee a originale should a have said had a dee a author known a what a we a all a know a today a about a Bushistotele: dat a—how a u a say?—dat a hine-a-sight, she a 20-20."

"But this is going to be presented to the pope!"

"Like a eye a say, whatta u a point?"

"That you're lying to the pope!"

"No a," Mrs. Irma R. Gorgonzola said. "Wee a no a lie. Dee a pope, he a berry old a man, so wee a tell a him whatta he a wanna hear. He a like a tings to a bee a certain a way, and a wee a give a him whatta he a want."

At this point Sister Naomi, who was for the second day running Lemon Pledging that dusty oversized St.-Francis-of-Assisi-holding-a-vicious-looking-squirrel-in-his-arms statue that was pleasantly tucked away in a distant corner, shuffled toward us. She eavesdropped as she began Lemon Pledging the wainscoting that paneled the lower portion of Mrs. Irma R. Gorgonzola's office's walls.

"Now a, Stefano," Mrs. Irma R. Gorgonzola continued, "Eye a no a wanna no a trouble wit a u, but u a have a to a unnerstand: wee a have a job a to a do, and a dat job is a to a *tradurre*—how a u a say? 'a trans a late'—dee a history of a Bushistotele. But a dis a translation, itta have to be in a certain a way a: dee a philosophy of a Bushistotele, itta dove-a-tail a nicely wit a much a of a dee a Catolic a doctrine—*capisci?*—so a dee a history, itta got a be true a to a our a doctrine. Dats a what a dee a *papa*, he a expecting. *Capisci?*"

"*Sì*," I told Mrs. Irma R. Gorgonzola. "*Capisco. Ma non è anche vero che devo seguire la lettera dell'originale?*"

"*Cosa dici?*"

"*Ma non è anche vero che devo seguire la lettera dell'originale?*"

"*Cosa?*"

"*MA NON È ANCHE VERO CHE DEVO SEGUIRE LA LETTERA DELL'ORIGINALE?*"

"Speak a dee a English, please," Mrs. Irma R. Gorgonzola said. "Eye a born in a Brooklyn and a eye a no a unnerstand a u. And eye a no a deaf, eeder."

I translated: "But isn't it also true that I should follow the letter of the original?"

"Wee a no a wanna no a more a blasphemy. No a more a Apocrypha: wee a have a enough a problems wit a dee a Dead a Sea a Scrolls. Dee a Holy a Fadder, he a no a like a peeples to a contradict a him, and he a no a like *i manoscritti* dat a contradict dee a *versione ufficiale da Roma*. So a dee a story of a Bushistotele, itta have a to a conform a, too a."

"But Mrs. Gorgonzola," I protested. "I'm not so sure that I can be a party to changing history!" Then, suddenly and uncharacteristically overcome by scruples, I shouted: "And it's immoral, too!"

"Dis a bee a why a wee a have a dee a problems wid a dee a—how a u a say a? *i traduttori*—inna dee a past. Dey no a like a to change a dee a words of a Bushistotele. Dats a why a all a of a our a ancient Greeks a here a bee a dead."

"Are you saying that it killed the other translators to change the words of Bushistotle like it kills me?"

"Not a exactly," said Mrs. Irma R. Gorgonzola. "Dee a *Vaticano*, wee a bee a country, u a know? So a wee a control a who a come a inna, and who a go a out. Iffa wee a no a like a u, u a donna a leave. *Capisci?*" Mrs. Irma R. Gorgonzola winked.

"You hold me prisoner?"

Mrs. Irma R. Gorgonzola shook her head no, then she made a slicing motion across her neck with her finger. I got her point: it might have been the Vatican, but how far is Sicily from Rome?

Irma motioned Sister Mary Subjugation over. "U a tink about a it," Irma said. "Dee a Sister here a, she a take a u a back a to a u a cell, so a u a can a tink about it." With that, Sister Mary Subjugation—whose real nun-name I hadn't yet learned—grabbed me by the ear and dragged me out of Irma's office, down the hall and back to my cell.

"Oooouch!" I kept yelling. "Oooouch! But I can't support Bushistotle! Oooouch! I'd rather die!" But she would not let me go.

So much had changed since Irma's lighthearted email claiming "Wee knead a you!": an adventure that had started with such promise saw me imprisoned somewhere deep inside the Vatican, with no way to contact the outside world for help. Now I was kept for days in my cell with no food and very little water, though exactly how many days I cannot say. I shed pounds (which has its pluses, but not like this), and I was convinced that I was coming down with scurvy. I was definitely coming down with halitosis. Then one morning I awoke to find that someone had stuffed a stale chocolate croissant—yum, chocolate!—under my door. It was crushed nearly flat, with the chocolate squished out the ends, and it had lost its characteristically appealing crescent shape, but it was a treat nonetheless. Fortunately, unlike in the movies, there were no rats or roaches nibbling at the ends of it, so I didn't feel like Papillion. I shoved it in my mouth all at once, swallowed it as best I could, pushed it down with some more of that rancid Roman water: if this is what they make the holy stuff out of, it's no wonder it kills evil spirits! I swallowed just in time, too, because Sister Mary Subjugation thereafter pounded on the door, and barged right in.

She stopped in her tracks, wiggled her nose like a dog smelling the air just as you start carving the Thanksgiving turkey because he wants some; in Sister Mary Subjugation's case, she must have smelled the chocolate. But the evidence was swallowed so she could do nothing about it; she merely gesticulated at me that it was time to get back to work. I made sure not to open my mouth until the chocolate had dissolved off my teeth, but halfway to the Secret Archives I could no longer contain myself. "Can I go to the bathroom, please?" I asked Sister Mary Subjugation. "I just can't do it in a bedpan. Nothing comes out."

Sister Mary Subjugation sighed, led me down another hallway, and despite the *Uomini* sign on the door pushed it open and entered along with me; I guess she didn't want to leave me alone. But let me tell you: the sight of a nun in the boy's room sure is enough to get a guy's adrenaline going, even in the Vatican! Pants zipped up, cassocks pushed down, zoom, zoom, men were flying everywhere, headed straight out the door! Though I only caught the last of it, it seems there was a mighty lot of communion going on in that bathroom, but not all of it was legit. Boys after all will be boys, and priests will be priests, but Sister Mary Subjugation just nodded her head in disgust.

Briefly overcome by a Borsht-Belt moment, I invented a private joke: *How many priests can you fit in one bathroom stall?* Unfortunately the punch line—*Lots!*—wasn't nearly as funny as the joke itself, and as I tried to figure out how to fix it another dozen or so clerics sped out of the stalls and past me, at least one of whom was cute. The coast clear, Sister Mary Subjugation checked the window to make sure it was bolted shut, then she gave me a moment of privacy.

I entered a stall, made ready to do my business, when a pair of smelly sandals that looked like they'd walked to Jerusalem and back by themselves, stuffed till they overflowed with fat feet clad in standard-issue white socks, of course bereft of elastic and falling to the ankles, appeared in the stall next to mine; someone must have been standing on the toilet to avoid being found by the Sister.

Then a face peered from under: it was Fra Diavolo!

"Can I have a moment to myself?" I asked.

"Sorry," said Fra Diavolo's upside-down head, which promptly disappeared. "I thought you might be a priest."

"No," I answered. "They all ran out when the nun came in."

"Damn nuns! You're the Greek translator, aren't you?"

"Yes."

"Trust no one."

"Okay."

"Be discreet."

Then I farted, but I couldn't help myself: gas builds up when you don't eat, and have nothing but a bedpan to crap in.

"Discreet!" Fra Diavolo said. "Do as you're told, but don't."

"Okay," answered I, and I tried to concentrate on my business.

"You are in mortal danger."

This was so Deep Throat!

I finished my business as fast as I could (which after several days of not crapping was fast), and as you can imagine I felt a great relief. Alas, Sister Mary Subjugation was waiting for me in the hallway, which put a quick end to my brief state of relief: she checked my hands and made me go back inside to wash them because apparently my nails were dirty, and if anybody would know about dirty nails it'd certainly have to be her. Afterward it was our fast march down the corridors and into the Vatican Secret Archives' Isolation Booth. Fra Diavolo was not at the Reference Desk yet; I figured he'd made another friend in the *uomini*'s room. Sister Naomi then arrived with a silver tray of coffee and what appeared to be Krispy Kreme donuts. Gosh how I love jelly donuts! Italy has great pastries, it's true, but not a cannole in the world can beat a juicy jelly donut in my book, and you can just about only get them in America!

The tray rattling in her unsteady old hands, Sister Naomi looked at the Windex blotches on the manuscript, mumbled "achim sadoc abiud amon zorobabel" to me again, which reflated back into English meant, "Sorry about that," and she placed the tray before me.

"I need to talk to you, Sister Naomi," I said, but Sister Mary Subjugation pointed at the door: she would have none of it!

Sister Naomi mumbled "achim sadoc abiud amon zorobabel" to me, which this time meant that I was not allowed to talk to anyone, nor was she. She exited the Isolation Booth walking backwards, never turning her face away from the other nun.

I reached for the coffee but Sister Mary Subjugation would not let me; she began to eat the donuts and drink the coffee that Sister Naomi had brought; I thought I spied a sadistic Mona Lisa smile on her, but perhaps I was mistaken, as jelly ringed her unmade-up face. I looked down at the Windex-splotched parchment, decided to skip over this difficult part for now and work on something easier. I used a time-tested technique of translators everywhere when they don't want to be bothered trying to figure out handwriting: I typed [illegible text] and advanced a page or two, where the writing was clearer, and where I found Bushistotle explaining his Theory of Everything to a very compliant Dudley the Donkey.

""""*The world is binarial," explained Bushistotle, the Philosopher-Warrior-King of Athens. Dudley the Donkey, bemused, sat on the bench alongside of Mrs. Bushistotle.*

""""*"What does bemused mean?" Mrs. Bushistotle asked Bushistotle, the Philosopher-Warrior-King of Athens.*

""""*"I don't know," answered Bushistotle, the Philosopher-Warrior-King of Athens. "You wrote this book, not me!"*

""""*"Oh!" said Mrs. Bushistotle, "I guess I did!"*""

I interpreted this brief metapassage in <u>Dudley the Donkey Learns a Lesson</u> as a quasi-literary attempt by Mrs. Bushistotle to assert her intellectual superiority over Bushistotle himself, the legendary

Philosopher-Warrior-King of Athens, but Bushistotle was never a man to be outdone by his wife. """"Do you know, Mrs. Bushistotle," asked Bushistotle, the Philosopher-Warrior-King of Athens, "why binarialism is the basis of our Republican philosophy?"

""""Why no, I don't!" she answered.

""""What about you, Dudley?" asked Bushistotle, the Philosopher-Warrior-King of Athens.

"Dudley the Donkey brayed sadly.

""""It's because the world is binarial," said Bushistotle, the Philosopher-Warrior-King of Athens, "which means that everything can be expressed as polar opposites. You have good or bad, black or white, dog or cat, and so on and so forth. We represent 'good' or 'right' as a one." Bushistotle, the Philosopher-Warrior-King of Athens, then held up his left index finger. "And we represent 'bad' or 'wrong' as a zero." Bushistotle, the Philosopher-Warrior-King of Athens, then held up his right hand, and made a circle with his thumb and index finger. "He'" — "that would be me, Bushistotle," Bushistotle said — "proceeded to insert his left index finger — the "one" — into the circle he had made with his right index finger and thumb — the "zero" — in rapid-fire succession. "This is what we do to the world: unite it!"

"Dudley the Donkey brayed in happiness!

""""You mean 'male' and 'female,'" said Mrs. Bushistotle. "Now I understand!"

""""Yes," said Bushistotle, the Philosopher-Warrior-King of Athens, still rapidly inserting his left index finger into the circle formed with his right index finger and thumb. "The next question, of course, is do you know why one equals male and zero equals female and not the other way around?" he asked as he continued inserting his finger in rapid-fire succession.

"Dudley the Donkey brayed in happiness, then jumped onto Bushistotle, the Philosopher-Warrior-King of Athens, and began to hump his leg.

""""Down, Dudley, down!" cried Bushistotle, the Philosopher-Warrior-King of Athens. "That's not the answer! Down!" Dudley the Donkey returned to his seat, and Bushistotle, the Philosopher-Warrior-King of Athens, adjusted his suit. "The correct answer is that it's because of what we call 'Bushistotlism': the opposite sexes are meant to be joined together, because they fit," said Bushistotle, the Philosopher-Warrior-King of Athens. "Bushistotlism' is the basis of our Family Values!""

Here Sister Mary Subjugation interrupted me by nodding her head no. More like, "No! No! No!" She then expurgated everything I had just translated, replacing it with "[illegible text]," and motioned me to proceed.

Fair enough, I thought, for a virgin, but I'm still not quite able to square deleting the fundamental basis of Bushistotle's Republican Philosophy—Family Values—with all the naked people painted on the Vatican's walls, since naked people are what you need to make a family, but given my hunger-induced enervated state, I was in no condition to argue. Rather, I continued with the ancient text:

Cheneyon interrupted Bushistotle. "Excuse me, Honorable Bushistotle," Cheneyon said, grabbing at Bushistotle's hands. "We need your decision regarding Sparta's attack on Syracuse!"

Realizing that *"grabbing at Bushistotle's hands"* would no longer make sense since Sister Mary Subjugation had [illegible texted] out the preceding part, I reviewed my translation. Nearly starved to death and with the smell of jelly donuts wafting around me, my stomach growled loudly. Then I took a very deep breath, put my hand on the backspace key, and did the theretofore unthinkable; I deleted a few things, changed a few more things until the text read: *"Cheneyon interrupted Bushistotle. 'Excuse me, Honorable Bushistotle,' Cheneyon said. 'We need your decision regarding Sparta's attack on Syracuse!'"*

I looked over at Sister Mary Subjugation, who showed no emotion. However, she passed me the last of the jelly donuts that was lying on the silver tray, and allowed me to sip what was left of the coffee. It felt so good to eat, but it felt so bad to emasculate the truth (and myself) just so I could get some food. Now, however, after many days locked down in a Vatican cell, and multiple calligraphic warnings that I was in danger, no doubt was left about what I needed to do to survive: join Task Force B.S. with all my heart, lie about Bushistotle, and make him into something he wasn't. The only question was whether I could do it, or whether I would just rather die.

Bushistotle agreed, I continued translating. *"Yes," he said, "we need a decision made. But I believe we have made a decision! If Spartan terrorists have attacked Athens at Syracuse, then Athens must attack Persia at... at... someplace inside of Persia!"*

"What about the capital of Persia?" asked Constantina.

"What a good idea!" said Bushistotle. "But what's the capital of Persia?"

"Persepolis," answered Constantina.

"Then I think we'll attack Persepolis," Bushistotle said. "I mean why not, right, if you can?"

"No!" interceded Rumsfeldiavelli. "It's too far inland, and only accessible via the Persian Gulf."

"Who cares?" said Bushistotle, waiving his arm derisively. "If the Spartans attacked us in Sicily, then the Persian Gulf is the last place they'd expect us to counterattack!"

"And counterattack against the Persians, too!" said Constantina gleefully. "What a surprise to the world!"

"Brilliant strategy, Honorable Bushistotle!" said Cheneyon. "We'll really catch the bunch of them off guard!"

"But the Persians didn't attack us!" said Powellonius.

"Shut up!" said Constantina. "We're attacking Persepolis!"

"No!" interceded Rumsfeldiavelli again. "Persepolis is too far away."

"Then where?" asked Bushistotle. "I'm running out of patience and I want to get back to <u>Dudley</u>."

"Byzantium," answered Ashcroftus. "Let's attack Byzantium! It's close by, and the population will welcome us with open arms!"

What a maroon! I thought.

"And then from there we can march straight to Persepolis, the capital," said Constantina. "We won't encounter any resistance whatsoever!"

Double maroon! I thought.

"Number One?" Bushistotle said to Cheneyon.

"It's doable, Chief," Cheneyon answered. "We'll be viewed by the world as liberators."

Triple maroon! I thought.

"Byzantium is entirely walled and heavily fortified," Powellonius said. "No one has taken it in a millennium!"

"But we have weapons," announced Rumsfeldiavelli.

"What kind?" asked Bushistotle.

"Well, Chief," answered Rumsfeldiavelli, "we have conventional, biological and chemical weapons that are unmatched anywhere in the civilized world."

"Weapons of Limited Destruction," said Cheneyon.

"As long as they're of Limited Destruction," said Bushistotle.

"And the Honorable Rumsfeldiavelli and I have worked out a plan," said Constantina.

"Oh, good!" said Bushistotle. "What's the plan?"

"Plagues," said Constantina.

"Please, Honorable Constantina!" interrupted Rumsfeldiavelli. "You were only tangential in preparing this plan. Chief, we have plagues. Ten in all, which will consist first of biowarfare: a red tide algae that will render all waters of the Golden Horn undrinkable. If this doesn't make the Persians surrender, then we will unleash another plague, one of yellow frogs."

"I hate yellow frogs," said Bushistotle.

"They will flourish in the swamps outlying Byzantium," said Rumsfeldiavelli.

"What's next?" asked Bushistotle.

"If the yellow frogs don't get them, then we have gnats, and if gnats don't get them, then flies."

"These are the nastiest of biological weapons, aren't they?" Bushistotle asked.

"You haven't heard the worst of it," said Ashcroftus.

"Then we have test tube after test tube of cattle plague," announced Rumsfeldiavelli, "just waiting to be strewn across their fields." Rumsfeldiavelli rubbed his hands together in joy.

"That is truly horrible!" said Bushistotle. "Wow!"

"It's talc!" cried Powellonius.

"Shut up!" said Constantina. "Just wait till I have your job!"

"Are you in favor, Honorable Bushistotle?" asked Ashcroftus.

"If it'll help us recapture Byzantium and advance our international agenda I am," Bushistotle pledged, "to spread freedom and liberty throughout the world through warfare!"

"I'm glad you're on board, Honorable Bushistotle," said Rumsfeldiavelli, "because if this biowarfare doesn't work, then we're moving to chemical, spreading some nasty stuff that will cause people and animals to break out in boils."

"How ugly!" cried Bushistotle.

"And if the biological and chemical stuff doesn't work," said Rumsfeldiavelli, "then we'll move to more traditional warfare with a blitzkrieg of firebombs like the biggest hailstorm you've ever seen."

"Wow!" said Bushistotle.

"And if they still don't surrender then it's back to biowarfare with locusts," said Rumsfeldiavelli. "We're breeding millions of them as we speak, and God are the hatchlings ugly."

"Truly shock and awe!" said Bushistotle. "But do we actually have all these weapons?"

"Ready to be deployed," said Cheneyon.

"Our next plague will be days of darkness, caused by large fires that we'll set in the outskirts of the city," said Ashcroftus.

"Wow!" said Bushistotle. "How many days?"

"We were leaning towards three days and three nights," answered Ashcroftus, "but it will depend on atmospheric conditions."

"The weather?" asked Bushistotle.

"Yes," said Rumsfeldiavelli.

"Understood," said Bushistotle.

"But the last one is the toughie," said Rumsfeldiavelli. "The destruction in one night of all the first-born. Though that's the idea, we're still in the planning stages, trying to figure out how to do it. We're thinking of landing a contingent of special operations forces to change the expiration dates on their baby formula right as it sits on store shelves, but we have plenty of time and nine WLD's to use before we reach it."

"Anyhow if it doesn't work we're considering a plague of cockroaches, just for good measure!" said Cheneyon.

"What a marvelous plan!" said Bushistotle.

"As if writ by the hand of God himself!" shouted Ashcroftus.

"Amen to that!" said Bushistotle. "Will these be enough to conquer Byzantium?"

"You have my guarantee," answered Rumsfeldiavelli.

"And it will make Sicily safe for Athenians," said Ashcroftus.

"But we have no right to invade," said Powellonius.

"No matter," Cheneyon said.

"We'll need an excuse for the attack," said Ashcroftus, "when we go public. A legal reason to justify our actions."

"Every nation has the right to self-defense," said Constantina.

"But we haven't been attacked by the Persians," said Powellonius.

"But they might attack," said Constantina.

"We must keep our gods safe from Ahura Mazda!" said Ashcroftus

"Ahura who?" Bushistotle asked.

"Ahura Mazda," answered Ashcroftus. "The Persian god, the god of Zoroaster."

"Isn't Zorro Astor a rich Mexican?" Bushistotle asked. "I think I met him at a fundraiser."

"He is a heathen prophet!" Ashcroftus said.

"Well then I deny meeting him at a fundraiser!" said Bushistotle.

"I concur with the Honorable Constantina," Cheneyon said. "In my opinion no reason is needed. You're always free to fight back when you're attacked."

"Honorable Gentlemen," Constantina said. "Although I don't think we

need a pretext for war, if we must have one then we will claim that the Persians have Weapons of <u>Mass</u> Destruction!"
"We have no hard evidence of that," said Powellonius.
"We know they want them!" said Constantina.
"Everyone wants them," said Powellonius.
"I support that," said Bushistotle. "I'm Macedonian, and everybody in Macedonia bears arms."
"Everybody but our enemies," reminded Cheneyon.
Bushistotle paused. "Oh yeah," he said. "That, too."

Here I stopped my translation because I could see it was not heading in a way that would please Sister Mary Subjugation. "I think this needs a little editing," I said. I took a deep breath. "Can I have a cup of coffee, please, Sister?"

Sister Mary Subjugation rose from her uncomfortable chair, exited the Isolation Booth, locking me in. No sooner had she left the room, however, than an Instant Message popped onto my screen: "Don't do it!"

I was startled: my own conscience sending me an Instant Message? How was that possible?

"Do what?" I typed back, but there was no response; nonetheless I decided to take advantage of Sister Mary Subjugation's absence since she thought I was on her side: I tried to send an email for help. First I tried AOL: "Website Unavailable" was the response. Damn! Then I tried Hotmail: "Website Unavailable," too. Damn! Then I tried every Internet domain I could think of, even vatican.com, holysee.biz, and papalstate.org, but they were all "Website Unavailable." Damn! So then I tried a chat room, to see if I could get a conversation going; first I tried one of the more innocent ones that I rarely ever logged onto because I had no real reason to. It was the same: "Website Unavailable." Damn! Then I tried a tawdrier site. "Website Unavailable" again. Damn! Then I tried the tawdriest site I knew: "Website Unavailable," yet again.

Damn! There was no way to communicate! What did all these bishops do with their free time if they couldn't use their PC's to cruise?

Presently I saw Sister Mary Subjugation returning to the Isolation Booth; I erased the messages just as she was unlocking the door. My heart pounded rapidly—what if she found out what I had done?

Once inside, she handed me a cup of coffee and a large piece of

Ghirardelli chocolate, I guess as a further prize for my cooperation. I tried to relax: my one attempt to get help was completely thwarted by the Vatican's firewall, so I would have to come up with a new plan.

The coffee and chocolate were scrumptious, but no analgesic for my pain. "Metapain," I called it: the pain suffered for inflicting pain upon others. The pain I inflicted on others by forcing them to believe things about Bushistotle that weren't true!

Anger rose in me; I looked at the ancient parchment, tore a section out. Sister Mary Subjugation gasped a silent-movie Gloria Swanson-type gasp, or swoon.

"Not to worry, Sister," I said. "You'll see."

I took the torn text and placed it elsewhere in the manuscript. My next step was to take some of my hot coffee and pour it on the manuscript; Sister Mary Subjugation looked aghast again, but refrained from miming another sigh. Then I tweaked the text here and there to make it more pro-Bushistotle, so that the heavily redacted and rewritten result, which would thenceforward become the true history of Bushistotle's campaign against Persia regardless of how fake it was, read from the top:

Bushistotle agreed. "Yes," he said, "we need a decision made. But I believe we have made a decision! If Spartan terrorists have attacked Athens at Syracuse aided and abetted by the Persians, then Athens must attack Persia! What plans do we have in place to attack Persia?"

"What about attacking Persepolis, the capital?" asked Constantina.

"No!" interceded Rumsfeldiavelli. "It's too far inland, and only accessible via the Persian Gulf."

"Then no!" said Bushistotle, waiving his arm. "But I need a plan. I'm running out of patience."

"Byzantium," answered Ashcroftus. "It's close by, and the population will welcome us with open arms!"

"And then from there we can march straight to Persepolis, the capital," said Constantina. "We won't encounter any resistance whatsoever!"

Some things you just can't edit out!

"Number One?" Bushistotle said to Cheneyon.

"It's doable, Chief," Cheneyon answered. "We'll be viewed by the world as liberators."

Ditto.

"Byzantium is entirely walled and heavily fortified," Powellonius said. "No one has taken it in a millennium!"

"But we have weapons," announced Rumsfeldiavelli.

"What kind?" asked Bushistotle.

"Well, Chief," answered Rumsfeldiavelli, "we have conventional, biological and chemical weapons that are unmatched anywhere in the civilized world."

"Weapons of Limited Destruction," said Cheneyon.

"As long as they're of limited destruction," Bushistotle said.

"But we'll need a reason for the attack," said Ashcroftus. "A legal reason to justify our actions."

"Every nation has the right to self-defense," said Constantina.

[illegible text: coffee stain]

"I concur with the Honorable Constantina," Cheneyon said.

[illegible text: Windex blotch]

"Honorable Gentlemen," Constantina said. "Although I don't think we need a pretext for war, we know that the Persians have Weapons of _Mass Destruction!_"

"Weapons of _Mass_ Destruction!" cried Bushistotle. "How horrible!"

"Indeed!" said Constantina.

"We have [illegible text] hard evidence of that," said Powellonius. "We have [illegible text] hard evidence of that!"

[illegible text: Windex blotch]

"Yes we do," said Constantina.

[illegible text: Windex blotch]

"What are they?" asked Bushistotle. "What Weapons of _Mass_ Destruction do these Persian dogs have? What is their plan?"

"Plagues," said Constantina.

"Chief, they have plagues," said Rumsfeldiavelli. "Ten in all, which will consist first of biowarfare: a red tide algae that will render all waters undrinkable. If this doesn't make us surrender, then they will unleash another plague, one of yellow frogs."

"I hate yellow frogs," said Bushistotle.

"They will flourish in the swamps outlying Piraeus," said Rumsfeldiavelli.

"What's next?" asked Bushistotle.

"If the yellow frogs don't get us, then they have gnats, and if gnats don't get us, then flies."

"These are the nastiest of biological weapons, aren't they?" Bushistotle asked.

"You haven't heard the worst of it," said Ashcroftus.

"Then they have test tube after test tube of cattle plague," announced Rumsfeldiavelli, "just waiting to be strewn across our fields." [illegible text: Windex blotch]

"That is truly horrible!" said Bushistotle. [illegible text: Windex blotch]

[illegible text: coffee stain]

"If this biowarfare doesn't work," Rumsfeldiavelli said, "then they're moving to chemical, spreading some nasty stuff that will cause people and animals to break out in boils."

"How ugly!" cried Bushistotle [illegible text: Windex blotch].

"And if the biological and chemical stuff doesn't work," said Rumsfeldiavelli, "then they'll move to more traditional warfare with a blitzkrieg of firebombs like the biggest hailstorm you've ever seen."

"Awful!" said Bushistotle.

"And if we still don't surrender then it's back to biowarfare with locusts," said Rumsfeldiavelli. "They're breeding millions of them as we speak, and God are the hatchlings ugly."

[illegible text: Windex blotch] "But do they actually have all these weapons?" asked Bushistotle.

[illegible text: coffee stain]

"Their next plague will be days of darkness, caused by large fires that they'll set in the outskirts of the city," said Ashcroftus.

[illegible text: Windex blotch] "How many days?" asked Bushistotle.

[illegible text: Windex blotch] "Three days and three nights," answered Ashcroftus, "but it will depend on atmospheric conditions."

"The weather?" asked Bushistotle.

"Yes," said Rumsfeldiavelli.

"Understood," said Bushistotle.

"But the last one is the toughie," said Rumsfeldiavelli. "The destruction in one night of all our first-born. Though that's the idea, they're still in the planning stages, trying to figure out how to do it. They're thinking of landing a contingent of special operations forces to change the expiration dates on our baby formula right as it sits on store shelves, but they have plenty of time and nine WMD's to use before they reach it."

"Anyhow if it doesn't work they're considering a plague of cockroaches, just for good measure!" said Cheneyon.

"What an awful plan!" said Bushistotle.
[illegible text: Windex blotch]
"Will these be enough to conquer Athens?" asked Bushistotle.
"You have my guarantee," answered Rumsfeldiavelli.
"Then I am justified in making the decision to go to war?" asked Bushistotle.
"Yes!" answered the Plenary Coterie.
"When will our forces be ready?" asked Bushistotle.
"They are now, Chief," said Rumsfeldiavelli.
"Then bring 'em on!" Bushistotle cried.
"Hail Bushistotle!" shouted the Coterie. "Hail Bushistotle!"

And Sister Mary Subjugation applauded loudly at the resulting history of Bushistotle's campaign against Persia, which bore no resemblance to what had been written and what was commonly known to be the true history.

"You realize we're lying?" I said to her. "This is not at all what happened in Persia."

She shrugged her shoulders as if she didn't care. For my part, I felt very, very ill: maybe it was the residual ammonia from the Windex mixing with bitter Italian coffee and Ghirardelli chocolate on a near-empty stomach, but deep down I knew that it was something that I had done, like change the history of the world.

My "conversion" to Vatican orthodoxy made me extremely popular, at least at the Vatican: I was immediately given a free room upgrade to what I would classify as the "Vice-Presidential Cell," complete with its own 30-bottle wine cooler stuffed with yummy Christian Brothers sacramental wine, a constant supply of hors d'oeuvres served on what tasted like stale Eucharists rather than your standard run-of-the-mill Melba Toast, all piled on a tarnished silver tray atop an antique credence table. And, of course, the pièce de la résistance: a view, albeit of an interior courtyard. To get a real view I'd probably have to take Holy Orders, and since the likelihood of my becoming a priest was extremely low despite their better sex life, I figured I shouldn't complain.

Now I thought I was doing my part for Task Force B.S., and hoped to be left alone. Secretly I even thought that compliance might win my release. It came as a shock, then, when one morning Sister Naomi mumbled "achim sadoc abiud amon zorobabel" to me, which reflated back into English meant that a gala dinner was to be given in my honor the next week, and that I would be reading a speech.

Nearly speechless at the thought of giving a public speech (my last public appearance had been in college drama class, where I was chosen to play a tree), at night in the Vice-Presidential Cell, in between indulgences of fantasy centered on myself and one particular male nude painted on the ceiling above my bed, where a lesser, non-Italian decorator might have tastelessly affixed a smoked-glass mirror, I cogitated about what I would say to the assembled crowd. Most of the time nothing of particular interest came to mind except, again, that male nude above me, but one night, and rather suddenly I would say, I was filled with inspiration that must have come from the Holy Ghost him- and/or itself, because it certainly didn't come from me.

In this inspiration I thought to utter these words, which departed my lips not unlike other people's Tongues, to the persons that would be sitting before me: "For that is rightly called fallacious which has a certain appetite of deceiving; which cannot be understood as without a soul: but this results in part from reason, in part from nature; from reason, in rational creatures, as in men; from nature, in beasts, as in the fox. But what I call mendacious proceeds from those who utter falsehood, who in this point differ from the fallacious insofar as all the fallacious seek to mislead. But not everyone who utters falsehood wishes to mislead; for both mimes and comedies and many poems are full of falsehoods, rather with the purpose of delighting than of misleading, and almost all those who jest utter falsehood, but he is rightly called fallacious whose purpose is that someone should be deceived. But those who do not aim to deceive, but nevertheless feign somewhat, are mendacious only, or if not even this, no one at least doubts that they are to be called pleasant falsifiers."

These profound words—which as I said happened upon me of a sudden—described exactly what I felt, albeit pompously, and provided full justification for my confabulations and other translative inventions. Moreover, they were words of reprobation against the viciously deceptive actions being taken by Mrs. Irma R. Gorgonzola and Sister Mary Subjugation: subverting the spirit of my not-quite-accurate translation of the ancient texts in order to mislead the world into believing that Bushistotle was great when, in fact, he was not. This because whereas my original intent was no more than to utter a mendacity or two all in good jest—or, in my previous, "inspired" words, "rather with the purpose of delighting than of misleading"— to demonstrate further to myself and my friends what we already knew to be true (that Bushistotle was an idiot), Mrs. Gorgonzola and Sister Mary Subjugation were operating fallaciously because their purpose was that the world should be deceived into believing that Bushistotle was a visionary leader when he was not, and denying it the well-deserved opportunity to laugh (at him).

Call it splitting hairs if you want but it worked for me, and I was ready to stand up and state my piece. So I was stunned when Mrs. Irma R. Gorgonzola entered the Isolation Booth one day and said, "Here a bee a u a speech!" because "my a speech" were words that I had translated, and they consisted of Bushistotle's announcement to the Athenian people that war had been declared on Persia!

I protested. "But Mrs. Irma R. Gorgonzola!" I cried. "I can't say this!"

"Dey a bee a u a words," she said. "Udderwise, u a go a back a to a u a cell."

So my orders were clear: read the speech, or starve. I didn't know what to make of it, or what the purpose was; perhaps it was a rite of passage, but it felt more like an ordeal: if I could make my way through it and read the entire speech, then it would be considered Divine Intervention and proof of the veracity of my conversion. If I faltered, or stuttered, or refused or threw up, then it would be considered proof of the falsity of my conversion. The effect on me, however, would be to convert my eensie peccadillo of mendacity into one big fat mortal sin of fallaciousness!

On the appointed day Sister Mary Subjugation escorted me into the Vatican Cafeteria, I mean Refectory, which was full to the brim with nuns and priests and cardinals and laypeople, and perhaps another slave or two because at the Vatican you can't tell. I was seated at the dais, between a lectern to my left and Mrs. Irma R. Gorgonzola to my right. Sister Mary Subjugation sat on the other side of the dais beside Cardinal Bernie himself, leader of Task Force B.S.

Mrs. Irma R. Gorgonzola stepped up to the lectern, and Sister Mary Subjugation stood and placed herself at the far end of the dais; as Mrs. Gorgonzola spoke, Sister Mary Subjugation interpreted her words into sign language, I assume for any clergy who had taken a vow of deafness. "Brudders a, sisters a, fadders a, mudders a, and a loyal a lay a peeples like a me," Irma began. "Welcome to a dis a berry important a reading given by a dee a newest member of a our a team, dee a—how a u a say?—*traduttore ufficiale*, Mr. a Steven a Hanley."

Mrs. Irma R. Gorgonzola returned to her seat but Sister Mary Subjugation remained in her place, apparently to continue interpreting for the avowed deaf. When I stood the applause I received was tepid at best—limited, in fact, to Fra Diavolo—which I thought was rather rude considering all that I had sacrificed in the name of Catholic orthodoxy. "These," I began, "are the immortal words of the Honorable Bushistotle, the Philosopher-Warrior-King of Athens, which he spoke at the Acropolis to the citizens of his city-state, to explain to them his just rationale for declaring war on Persia:

"*My fellow Athenians: September 11, 350 BC—a date which will live in infamy—Athens was suddenly and deliberately attacked by naval and ground forces from the city-state of Sparta.*

"*Athens was at peace with that city-state and, at the solicitation of Sparta, was still in conversation with its Government and its Philosopher-King looking toward the maintenance of peace in the Mediterranean. Indeed, one hour after Spartan squadrons had commenced their assault on* the Athenian colony of Syracuse, the Spartan Ambassador to Athens and his colleague delivered to the Honorable Powellonius a formal reply to a recent Athenian message. While this reply stated that it seemed useless to continue the existing diplomatic negotiations, it contained no threat or hint of war or armed attack.

"'It will be recorded that the distance of Syracuse from Sparta makes it obvious that the attack was deliberately planned many days or even weeks ago. During the intervening time the Spartan Government has deliberately sought to deceive Athens by false statements and expressions of hope for continued peace.

"'The attack yesterday on the island of Sicily has caused severe damage to Athenian naval and military forces. Very many Athenian lives have been lost. In addition Athenian ships have been reported attacked on the high seas between Piraeus and Syracuse.

"'Yesterday the Spartan Government also launched an attack against Crete. Last night Spartan forces attacked Macedonia. Last night Spartan forces attacked Corinth. Last night Spartan forces attacked Thebes. Last night Sparta attacked Argos. This morning the Spartans attacked Lesbos, but in my opinion that's one island they can keep.

"Now none of this is remotely true, of course, which is what makes this Spartan offensive a surprise to most of the Mediterranean. The facts of September 11 speak for themselves, and therefore must be distorted. The people of Athens have already formed their opinions and well understand the implications to the very life and safety of our city-state, which is why we must spin these events.

"'Therefore, regardless of what Athenians think, or what might be a good idea, as Philosopher-now-Warrior-King, Commander-in-Chief of the Army and Navy of Athens, and Headmaster at the Athens Academy of Philosophy and Warfare soon to be renamed the Bushistotle Center, I have ordered that war be declared on Persia, in retaliation against the Spartans. Clever idea, ha? At this hour, Athenian forces and I think five lonely coalition soldiers are in the early stages of military operations to disarm Persia even though it has no arms, to free its people from tyranny as if that were our job, and to defend the world from the grave danger that exists only in my mind.

"'On my orders, coalition forces have begun striking selected targets in the Persian city of Byzantium to undermine Persia's ability to wage war. These are opening stages of what will be a broad and concerted campaign, ending only when we reach Persepolis and beyond. More than 35 countries are giving crucial support consisting of at least one soldier each, who they *promise are on their way, walking. Every nation in this coalition has chosen to bear the duty and share the honor of serving in our common defense against this fiercely imaginary enemy.*

"'To all the men of the Athenian Armed Forces now attacking Persia, the peace of a troubled world and the hopes of an oppressed people now depend on you. That trust is well placed. The enemies you confront will come to know your skill and bravery. The people you liberate will witness the honorable and decent spirit of the Athenian military. In this conflict, Athens faces an enemy who has no regard for conventions of war or rules of morality, making this also a major part of our greater offensive, the Culture War!

"'Intelligence invented by this and the one other like-minded government we've been able to find leaves no doubt that the evil Saladin's Persian Regime continues to possess and conceal some of the most lethal weapons ever devised, even if that's not true. Facing overwhelming amounts of falsified evidence of peril, we cannot wait for the final proof, the smoking gun that could come in the form of poisonous mushrooms, because we'll never find it. Rather, we must jump the gun. The current situation is a grave and gathering danger, and a mortal threat to my reelection prospects: already Athenian intelligence has fabricated the story that the Persians' Weapons of <u>Mass</u> Destruction consist of plagues, ten in all, which will consist first of biowarfare: a red tide algae that will render all our waters undrinkable. We also know that the Persian government has made overtures to buy yellow frogs from African nations, which will flourish in the swamps outlying Piraeus, and crowd out our native species. Then, like the French, we will be forced to eat frogs' legs, though we will call them "Freedom Legs."

"'If eating yellow frog ... Freedom ... legs doesn't get us, then the Persians have gnats, and if gnats don't get us, then flies: it's a really nasty country! Worse still, our intelligence officers have found trailers full of what we claim is cattle plague, or else talc, just waiting to be strewn across our fields. If this biowarfare doesn't work, then the Persians will move to chemical weapons, spreading some nasty stuff that will cause people and animals to break out in boils. And if the biological and chemical stuff doesn't work, then they'll move to more traditional warfare with a blitzkrieg of firebombs like the biggest hailstorm you've ever seen. And if we still don't surrender then it's back to biowarfare with locusts. They're breeding millions of them as we speak, and God are the hatchlings ugly. Their next plague will be many days of darkness—how many we're not sure of yet, but three days and three nights seems like a safe bet—caused by large fires that they'll set in the outskirts of the city. And the last of their plagues is the worst of all: the destruction in one

night of all our first-born by changing the sell-by dates on our store-bought baby formula!

"'This we know as baseless in fact, so I want Athenians and all the world to be certain that coalition forces will make every effort to spare our innocent civilians from harm, though their innocent civilians can go to hell because they started it. A campaign on the harsh terrain of a large nation like Persia could be longer and more difficult than some predict, but we'll ignore that fact for now. And helping Persians achieve a united, stable and free country will require our sustained commitment, and loads of money to be earned from cornering the market and selling their olive oil.

"'We come to Persia with respect for its citizens, for their great civilization and for the religious faiths they practice, which must be obliterated. We have no ambition in Persia except to take it over, remove a threat to nobody, and restore control of that country to some of its own people who we like better. And finally, of course, to take over its olive farms, for a reason which we will deny: we self-indulgent Athenians like our fried food!

"I know that the families of our military are praying that all those who serve will return safely and soon from this reckless crusade I have undertaken. Millions of Athenians are praying with you for the safety of your loved ones and for the protection of the innocent. For your sacrifice, you have the gratitude and respect of the Athenian people. Big deal, right? And you can know that our forces will be coming home as soon as their work is done, however many decades that takes.

"'Our nation enters this conflict reluctantly—but I do not. In fact, I relish the thought of being a wartime Philosopher-King, because it's the only way I can add "Warrior" to the title. The people of Athens and our friend and ally will not live at the mercy of Saladin's outlaw regime that threatens the peace with Weapons of <u>Mass</u> Murder. We will meet that threat now with our Army and Navy and our Weapons of Limited Murder, so that we do not have to meet it later with armies of fire fighters and police and doctors on the streets of our cities.

"'Now that we have sought conflict, I mean now that conflict has come, the only way to limit its duration is to apply decisive force. And I assure you, this will not be a campaign of half-measures, and we will accept no outcome but victory. In other words we're gonna bomb the shit out of them. My fellow citizens, the dangers to our country and the world will be overcome, and thereafter we will invent more. We will pass through this time of peril and carry on the work of peace. We will defend our freedom. We will bring freedom to others by force and we will prevail.

"'A great people has been moved to defend a great city-state, and the oppressed people of Persia will know the generosity of Athens once we annihilate them. Spartan attacks can shake the foundations of our biggest buildings and our most distant colonies, but they cannot touch the foundation of Athens. These acts shattered iron, but they cannot dent the iron of Athenian resolve.

"'Athens was targeted for attack because of our Republican Ideals: we think we're the brightest beacon for freedom and opportunity in the world. And no one will keep that light from shining. Yesterday, when the Spartans attacked us, our city-state saw evil, the very worst of human nature. And by declaring war against Persia in retaliation, we responded with the best of Athens: complete illogicalness, and our armed forces.

"'Immediately following the first attack, I implemented our government's emergency response plans, which means that I went into hiding, and couldn't be found for days. But our military is powerful, and it's prepared. Our first priority is to save my neck, and to take every precaution to protect me at home and around the world from further attacks. Our second priority is based on that sign from the Old West—Wanted Dead or Alive!—and you know what that means.

"'The functions of our government continue without interruption, entirely geared to this end. Thank God our financial institutions remain strong, and my money safe, so the Government can borrow endlessly from me at high interest rates to pay for this. The Athenian economy will be open for business, as well: war causes boom times and economic bubbles, and me and my Republican buddies are heavily invested in the market.

"'As I said, because we know that the Spartans are behind these evil acts and the Persians have nothing to do with it, and because we make no distinction between them and anybody else we don't like, we have launched this invasion of Persia. Athens and our friend and ally join with all those who want peace in the world by declaring war, and we stand together to win not only this War against the Spartans, but that far greater danger, the Culture War. Tonight, I ask for your prayers for them and all those who won't pray for themselves, or those who do pray but whose prayers go unanswered because God doesn't approve of their lifestyles. I pray they will be comforted by a power greater than any of us, spoken through the ages: "Even though I walk through the valley of the shadow of death, I fear no evil, for You are with me, and my fat white ass ain't there in Persia, and neither are my kids."

"'This is a day when all Athenians from every walk of life unite in our *resolve for justice and peace by waging an unnecessary war. Athens has stood down invented enemies before, and we will do so this time. None of us will ever forget that fateful September day in 350 BC. Yet we go forward to defend freedom and all that is good and just in our world."*

This should have been the end of it, but I turned the page and saw that underneath there was more. I hesitated; the crowd grew anxious, yet what I saw amazed me: more parchment folios filled with ancient Greek text, with a yellow Post-It Note stuck on top that said, "These were removed from the original text," again in bright calligraphic writing.

My heart fluttered; I looked up at the crowd. I rolled up Bushistotle's speech along with the new Greek text, and placed them in my pocket. Then I took a deep breath, looked out at the crowd again and said, *"Thank you. Good night, and God bless Athens!"*

The applause was uproarious; I had gotten through my ordeal! The crowd was on its feet, but just as I was about to thank them again for their kindness, this time in my own voice, they raised their chalicefuls of sacramental wine and shouted, "HAIL BUSHISTOTLE! HAIL BUSHISTOTLE! HAIL BUSHISTOTLE!" though for the life of me I couldn't figure out why.

Once I had returned to my seat Mrs. Irma R. Gorgonzola leaned toward me, whispered: "U a did a berry good a ting wit a u speech. Dee a *cardinale*, he a gonna bee a berry pleased a wit a u. Most a peeples, dey a choke a when a dey have a to speak dee a words of a Bushistotele. Itta make a dem sick, unless u a believe a inna what a Bushistotele he a stand a for. And iffa u a bee a true a believer, den a dee a words, dey a just a flow a from a u a mout." Mrs. Irma R. Gorgonzola gesticulated munificently with her arms as she said this, spreading them wide as if she were saying, *Behold the words of Bushistotle: A river of gold!* Then she added parenthetically: "But a for a me, eye a no a canna do it, because he a make a me a barf."

After my ordeal, I was exhausted. In fact, I had to be helped back to the Vice-Presidential Cell because I was unable to walk on my own. Some people might have found that embarrassing at my relatively middle age, but honestly there are worse fates in life than being helped down a hallway by a couple of hot young soldiers, even if they are the Vatican Swiss Guard. Naturally, I thanked the pair profusely when we arrived, invited them in for some sacramental Christian Brothers wine and leftover Eucharist hors d'oeuvres, but they politely declined. You can't fault me for trying, though.

Once securely inside I turned the too-dim dime-store light on, took the copy of my speech and the Mystery Text out of my pocket and set to read it, but not without noting that a brand new crucifix had been affixed to my cell wall, and a *Divieto di Usare Telefonini* sign had been Scotch-taped next to it: it was nice to see that someone was looking out for me!

Just by reading the first few words of the Mystery Text I was able to see how damning these expurgated pages would be to Bushistotle's reputation as a decisive leader; it seems, according to the original ancient text at least, or at least to my freely translated English version of it which admittedly might bear no resemblance whatsoever to said original text, that before Bushistotle would declare war on the Persians he consulted Cassandra, the infamous oracle of Troy who to no avail warned the Trojans not to let that damned horse into the city, but when he did not get the answer he was after he went oracle shopping, until he found one who gave him the answer he wanted to hear:

Bushistotle, the Philosopher-Warrior-King of Athens, dressed as a country bumpkin in his cowboy crown and boots, took the next vessel to Troy, to consult the mad oracle Cassandra. His error, of course was that he insisted on traveling First Class, when a true country bumpkin should fit more aptly in steerage. "But Bushistotle, Philosopher-Warrior-King of Athens," said Mrs. Bushistotle as she was helping Bushistotle choose his clothes for the trip, "no honest-to-goodness country bumpkin would travel in First Class. Only rich people do. And they most especially wouldn't wear their cowboy crown! That will give you away to even the lowliest of ticket takers!"

"But Mrs. Bushistotle," said Bushistotle, the Philosopher-Warrior-King

of Athens. "I am a country bumpkin in name only! You know that I come from a long line of blue blood, I mean red blood: my father before me was Philosopher-Warrior-King of Athens, and my grandfather was a member of the Senate. It is good that the people think that I'm a country bumpkin, but I know whose side of things I'm on!"

Thus Bushistotle, unmoved by Mrs. Bushistotle's supplications, set off on his secret trip to Troy, dressed in his dude ranch best: chaps, cowboy boots, and cowboy crown. Upon arrival at Troy he showed his diplomatic passport, and whizzed right through Immigration and Customs. "How ya'll doin'? I'm just a regular old country bumpkin!" he said, but the crowd was not buying it.

Outside of Immigration Bushistotle was met by a gilded hansom cab, and was whisked off away from the crowds by a contingent of security forces on horseback and on foot. Soon he was in the company of the oracle Cassandra, who was sitting in her usual spot at the Troy Midtown Saloon, downing her second bottle of whisky for the day, holding court.

"I come for a prophesy on my plans to invade Persia," Bushistotle said to Cassandra, whose blonde hair was disheveled and whose breath stank like a still.

"I know what you're here for," Cassandra slurred back. "You're Bushistotle, the Philosopher-Warrior-King of Athens."

"Oh, no," said he. "I am just a country bumpkin."

"Right," spat Cassandra. "A country bumpkin, and Philosopher-Warrior-King of Athens."

"I don't know how he was ever elected!" said a patron.

"That's a long story," said a second.

"But the world is safer with Bushistotle as Philosopher-Warrior-King in office, isn't it?" Bushistotle asked rhetorically.

There was silence in response. Then, after a long swig of rotgut whisky, Cassandra the mad oracle cried out: "O wretched men! why rage you possessed, dragging this unfriendly horse, hasting to your last night and the end of the war and the sleep that knows no waking?"

"What?" said Bushistotle. "Can you translate, please? Are you calling me a horse? What horse?" Bushistotle looked out the window. "My horse is fine."

"Your war, hun," said Cassandra, wiping her mouth with her forearm. "It's a losing proposition any way you slice it."

"You're gonna get us all killed," said the first patron from before.

"You don't know what you're up against," said the second patron from before.

Bushistotle turned to the head of his security forces. "This woman *is blitzed out of her mind,"* he said. *"And these patrons are not a Friendly Crowd. Aren't you responsible for ensuring a Friendly Crowd?"*

"Sorry, Honorable Bushistotle," said the head of his security forces.

"Let's get out of here," said Bushistotle. "I think we need to ask a sober oracle, in front of a Friendly Crowd. Or better, in front of no crowd at all."

Thereafter Bushistotle traveled to Claros, and then to Didyma, to seek an oracle whose opinion he could agree with. When he was met by prophesies of loss and destruction again, he moved on to the Mother of All Oracles, the Oracle at Delphi, to consult Apollo concerning the success of the war he was undertaking. Alas, Bushistotle happened to come on one of the forbidden days; his consultation occurred when it was esteemed improper to give any answer from the oracle. Nonetheless, Bushistotle sent messengers to desire the priestess to do her office, but when she yet refused, on the plea of a labor law to the contrary, he went up himself, to wait.

Bushistotle sat himself down on the omphalus, the carved round stone at Delphi known as the belly-button of the world because it connected mankind to the gods, where he waited for the Oracle's day off to end. There there were no other patrons but him, because most people know not to go to a store when it's closed. To bide his time, then, he took out his trusty copy of <u>Dudley the Donkey Learns a Lesson</u> which he never traveled without, and began to read from where he had last left off. He read aloud, since he had never learned to read to himself: "He"' — *"that would be me, Bushistotle," Bushistotle said* — *"'proceeded to insert his left index finger* — *the "one"* — *into the circle he had made with his right index finger and thumb* — *the "zero"* — *in rapid-fire succession. "This is what we do to the world: unite it!"*

"'Dudley the Donkey brayed in happiness!

""'You mean 'male' and 'female,'" said Mrs. Bushistotle. "Now I understand!"

""'Yes," said Bushistotle, the Philosopher-Warrior-King of Athens, still rapidly inserting his left index finger into the circle formed with his right index finger and thumb. "Do you know why one equals male and zero equals female?" he asked as he continued inserting his finger in rapid-fire succession.

"'Dudley the Donkey brayed in happiness, then jumped onto Bushistotle, the Philosopher-Warrior-King of Athens, and began to hump his leg.

""'Down, Dudley, down!" cried Bushistotle, the Philosopher-Warrior-King of Athens. "That's not the answer! Down!" Dudley the Donkey returned to his seat, and Bushistotle, the Philosopher-Warrior-King of Athens, adjusted his suit. "The correct answer is Bushistotlism: one and zero, or male and

female," said Bushistotle, the Philosopher-Warrior-King of Athens. "Good or bad. Black or white. Dog or cat. Yes or no. Bushistotlism is the basis of our Family Values!"

""That is so wonderful my husband Bushistotle, Philosopher-Warrior-King of Athens!"

"Dudley the Donkey brayed in happiness again.

""Some people think it's inappropriate to draw a moral line," explained Bushistotle, the Philosopher-Warrior-King of Athens, to Mrs. Bushistotle and Dudley, who were still sitting on the back-porch bench on the Bushistotles' ranch in the Macedonian Outback, learning their Bushistotle Lesson. "Not me. For our children to have the lives we want for them, they must learn to say Yes to responsibility ... Yes to honesty."

""And No to prescription drugs!" exclaimed Mrs. Bushistotle.

""Exactly!" cried Bushistotle, the Philosopher-Warrior-King of Athens. "For most Athenians, life is a fabric of helping hands and good neighbors, bedtime stories and shared prayers, lovingly packed lunchboxes and household budget-balancing, tears wiped away, a precious heritage passed along. It is hard work and a little put away for the future."

""That is so very Normal Rockwell of you," Mrs. Bushistotle said. "And so maudlin!"

""Why thank you, Mrs. Bushistotle," said Bushistotle, the Philosopher-Warrior-King of Athens. "I believe everybody should be held responsible for their own personal behavior, which is why I propose a restoration of timeless values, and a renewal of our national purpose: warfare."

"Dudley the Donkey brayed again in happiness.

""This is where my opponents go wrong," said Bushistotle, the Philosopher-Warrior-King of Athens. "For they do not stand for timeless values."

"Dudley the Donkey brayed sadly.

""But Bushistotle, Philosopher-Warrior-King of Athens," said Mrs. Bushistotle. "What timeless values do you stand for, besides war?"

""Besides war—or alongside it—our timeless values are Truth, Goodness and the Athenian Way," said Bushistotle, the Philosopher-Warrior-King of Athens, "which we get from the words of our gods.""

"That would be me!" cried a voice from inside the cave at Delphi: it was none other than the Karen the Oracle at Delphi, who was eavesdropping on Dudley's Lesson.

"That's why I'm here!" Bushistotle shouted back to the Oracle. "Can you come out now and tell me how my war is going to work out?"

"It's my day off, big boy," shouted the Oracle. "Go home and come back tomorrow!"

"I can't go back to the Academy until I have an answer from you, Madam Oracle, for I have an undesired war that I'm just itching to declare, and time's a'wasting. I'll wait till you return to duty, unless I get the chance to change the labor laws first, that is: days off eat into profits."

"Enjoy yourself, babes!" said the Oracle. "I got some neat stuff to smoke first, you know, to get in the prophesying mood. Wanna toke?"

"No, thank you," said Bushistotle. "I've sworn off since my college days, when I did, or did not, inhale." Bushistotle resumed his reading again: ""But Mrs. Bushistotle," said Bushistotle, the Philosopher-Warrior-King of Athens. "I would think that you knew that our Republican Ideal is "One Nation Under the Gods."

""Oh, my Bushistotle, Philosopher-Warrior-King of Athens," said Mrs. Bushistotle. "You must be very careful, for there is much the gods have said that you will not like!"

""Nonsense," said Bushistotle, the Philosopher-Warrior-King of Athens. "Balderdash!"

""For instance," said Mrs. Bushistotle, "the gods have commanded that you shall not withhold overnight the wages of your day laborers."

""They did not!" cried Bushistotle, Philosopher-Warrior-King of Athens. "What about our wetbacks and ranch hands? Paying them every day would cut into my profits! My gosh, paying them at all cuts into my profits!""

"Gods got you there, didn't we, babes?" cried the Oracle from inside the cave.

"Will you come out now and take me away from reading my wife's book, please?" Bushistotle pleaded to the Oracle. "It's disturbing me."

"I told you, babes, I'm off duty right now," answered the Oracle. "Come back tomorrow. I got some serious drugs to do."

Bushistotle sighed, then read: ""And the gods have ordered us not to eat meat with the blood still in it," said Mrs. Bushistotle.

""I like my steak rare, practically mooing," said Bushistotle, the Philosopher-Warrior-King of Athens.

"Dudley the Donkey brayed in agreement.'"

"Ha!" cried the Oracle from inside the cave. "The gods won't even let you eat a decent cut of meat!"

"Shut up!" shouted Bushistotle. "You're starting to bother me now." Then Bushistotle read: ""So we'd better nix that one, too, ay, Mrs. Bushistotle?"

""I think so," said Mrs. Bushistotle. "But we must also consider that the gods have ordered us not to put on a garment woven with two different kinds of thread."

""'They did not!" shouted Bushistotle, the Philosopher-Warrior-King of Athens.""'

"Yes they did!" the Oracle cried from inside the cave. "And I bet your toga is a Dacron-polyester blend!"

"Shut up!" shouted Bushistotle, "before I go in there after you." Then he read: ""'Here's another," said Mrs. Bushistotle: "Slaves, male and female, you may indeed possess, provided you buy them from among the neighboring nations."

""'Like Persia?" asked Bushistotle, the Philosopher-Warrior-King of Athens. "I like that idea."

"Mrs. Bushistotle looked at him unhappily.

""'I guess those were the good ol' days," said Bushistotle, the Philosopher-Warrior-King of Athens. "But we can get practically the same effect by never raising the minimum wage, so I guess we can live with it."

""'Whoever curses his father or mother shall be put to death," said Mrs. Bushistotle.

""'I'm all for that one," said Bushistotle, the Philosopher-Warrior-King of Athens. "Those two daughters of ours are getting way too fresh!"

""'Whoever strikes a man a mortal blow must be put to death," said Mrs. Bushistotle.

""'Ditto on the 'Yes' column," said Bushistotle, the Philosopher-Warrior-King of Athens. "Hang 'em from the nearest tree!"

""'Do not exact interest from your countryman either in money or in kind," said Mrs. Bushistotle.

""'That's problematic," said Bushistotle, the Philosopher-Warrior-King of Athens. "All of our banker friends! I can see now that we'll have to pick and choose which ones of the gods' rules we want to follow, and which ones we just want to let fall by the wayside."

""'Be careful to observe all our statutes and decrees. We are the gods," said Mrs. Bushistotle to Bushistotle, the Philosopher-Warrior-King of Athens. "The gods have also said that."

""'Well....""'

Now the Oracle, stoned to near unconsciousness, exited the cave and stumbled toward Bushistotle, who at first did not see that she was naked. "Here's a prophesy for you," she said seductively. "Should a prince commit a sin inadvertently by doing one of the things which are forbidden by some commandment of God, and thus become guilty, if later he learns of the sin he committed, he shall bring as his offering an unblemished male goat.' Got any unblemished male goats on hand, babes?"

"Well I am a prince," said Bushistotle to the Oracle, "but I've never committed a sin inadvertently because I always do it on purpose." Then he saw that the Oracle was naked; he quickly returned his eyes to the book: ""'You shall not lie with a male as with a woman; such a thing is an abomination," said Mrs. Bushistotle.

""'That's a Big Fat Yes," said Bushistotle, the Philosopher-Warrior-King of Athens.""

"When a man has an emission of seed, he shall bathe his whole body in water and be unclean until evening," said the approaching Oracle. "Wanna purify yourself in yonder Castalia Spring with me?" The Oracle pointed, sat beside Bushistotle on the belly-button of the world, stroked his leg gently, then ran her hand up his toga; he wasn't wearing underwear.

Bushistotle, startled, stood, stepped back, returned to his wife's book: ""'If a man commits adultery with his neighbor's wife, both the adulterer and the adulteress shall be put to death," said Mrs. Bushistotle.'"

The Oracle, light beads of sweat trickling down her breasts, also stood, walked toward Bushistotle, matching his gait, until Bushistotle walked backwards into a tree, and the Oracle pinned him against it.

"Did you hear that, Oracle?" said Bushistotle. "If a man commits adultery with his neighbor's wife, both the adulterer and the adulteress shall be put to death."

The Oracle pressed her lips against Bushistotle's, released them and said, "But we're not neighbors, are we?"

Bushistotle tried to return to <u>Dudley the Donkey Learns a Lesson</u>, but, panicked, he repeated a passage he had already read: ""'Be careful to observe all our statutes and decrees. We are the gods," said Mrs. Bushistotle to Bushistotle, the Philosopher-Warrior-King of Athens.'"

Bushistotle then dropped the book, wrapped his arms around the naked Oracle at Delphi, and began to draw her with all his force into the temple, where they fell upon her pillows. They embraced, their temperatures rose, their hearts pounded and they writhed. Then, a shriek: "Bushistotle! Bushistotle! No, Bushistotle!"

"Oracle! Oracle!"

"Bushistotle! Bushistotle!"

Dudley the Donkey brayed in happiness, *thought Bushistotle, in a vain attempt to get his mind off things and to prevent this chance encounter* with the Oracle from ending way too soon. *Braaaaaaaay! he thought. Braaaaaaaay!*

"*Aaaaaahhhhh!*" *he shrieked.* "*Aaaaaahhhhh!*"

"*Aaaaaahhhhh!*" *she shrieked.*

"*Aaaaaahhhhh!*" *they shrieked.*

"*Aaaaaahhhhh!*"

After a moment, tired and overcome, the naked Oracle said to Bushistotle: "*My son, thou art invincible.*"

Bushistotle, taking hold of what she spoke, pulled his toga back down, declared he had received such an answer as he wished for, and that it was needless to consult the gods further: the outcome of the war against Persia was guaranteed. Among other prodigies that attended the departure of his army, the image of Dudley the Donkey, made of cedar, was seen to sweat in great abundance, to the discouragement of many. But after the encounter with the Oracle Bushistotle figured that, far from presaging any ill to him, it signified he should perform acts so important and glorious as would make all the asses of future ages labor and sweat to describe and celebrate them.

Having now read the expurgated "Temptation of Bushistotle" that had been slipped to me by an unknown person or persons as an attachment to my rehashed Bushistotle "I'm-reluctant-to-declare-war-but-gee-I-have-to" speech, I hid the purloined text as best I could underneath the silver tray that bore the leftover Eucharist hors d'oeuvres; in all my days in the Vice-Presidential Cell I had never known them to take away the older hors d'oeuvres, but rather just add new ones to the pile, so I figured it would be safe there, protected as it was by ptomaine spores or whatever. Then, once the manuscript was safely hid, my next task would be to figure out how to smuggle out a translation of it.

I continued to toil day after day, loyally toeing the Vatican's official St. Bushistotle lie, I mean line. Of course I was intermittently plagued by the moral matter regarding the rewriting history that I was engaged in, but as Napoleon Bonaparte—or was it Carolus Rovus?—is quoted as saying, "History is a set of lies we all agree upon." Ergo, since much of the Bushistotle legacy was in any case based on just that—big fat lies—I tried to justify my actions along those lines—that all I was doing was adding one more layer of lies on top of all the other ones—never mind that Napoleon was one of the most brutal dictators in the history of the world and Rovus one of the evilest propagandists, though neither was probably worse than the Borgia popes whose statues dotted the miles of corridors I commuted to work along on a daily basis. Yet with every word I translated I yearned to spread the truth about Bushistotle, or at least what I believed to be the truth based on my misreading of the ancient texts.

But the more I conformed to the official "St. Bushistotle" line and did my part to distort history, the more I was treated like a king: grapes in my cell and oranges for my scurvy, spaghetti and meatballs every night, and of course my Krispy Kreme jelly donuts, which none other than the pope himself had ordered be flown in fresh from New York every day. (I was blowing up like a blimp and briefly considered low-carbs, but jelly donuts were the only real solace I had.) Outwardly I was expanding but inwardly I was shriveling because I wanted to spread the truth: what I was doing went against everything that I had ever thought I stood for, but it was the only real way to survive, because let's face it: jail makes you fat.

As the days elapsed the coldness I had heretofore felt when I entered the Isolation Booth where I worked in the Vatican Secret Archives also seemed to melt, and though I was still not allowed to talk to anyone I didn't feel that gazes were piercing me as Sister Mary Subjugation escorted me to my post. Fra Diavolo, for his part, developed a penchant for winking at me which was starting to get on my nerves; I didn't know how I'd break the news to him that the tonsured look was not something that I found appealing, never mind his brown horsehair frock, rope belt, and dilapidated Jerusalem sandals. Obviously I would have to avoid hanging out at the Reference Desk.

Over time my affair with Sister Mary Subjugation took a turn for the better, as well: she let me sleep in a little later, and let me go back to my cell a little earlier, and she granted me some additional degree of freedom, occasionally allowing me to stroll about the Secret Archives, and eventually even to talk to some of the researchers there, and to gaze in awe at how well endowed some of the nudes on the wall were: leave it to Michelangelo! What was not allowed, however, was to discuss the nature of my assignment, not even with anyone who might be a co-member of my team. Indeed, the only one who seemed to know exactly what was going on with Task Force B.S.—the Bushistotle Beatification Task Force, that is—was Cardinal Bernie himself, and he had not divulged the names of any other fellow Task Force B.S. members to me, nor had he explained the full scope of its mission. Until, that is, our second staff meeting, when Sister Mary Subjugation brought me in to see him.

"Great job on that speech, Steve!" he boomed, hand stretched out in front of him. "Most people couldn't have gotten through so much drivel without choking someplace along the way."

"You mean Bushistotle's, I mean the Honorable Bushistotle's, 'I'm-reluctant-to-declare-war-but-gee-I-have-to' speech?" I threw in the "Honorable" just in case he had some Ghirardelli chocolate; I was becoming a real whore.

"Of course!" he said. "You have an acting background?"

"I was a front-row tree in my college drama class."

"That's just the kind of experience you need for a job like this. Well done! Well done!"

"Thank you, Your Eminence."

"Bernie," the cardinal corrected. "Like I said, just call me 'Bernie.' Everyone does."

"Thank you, Bernie."

"Now I have some things to show you, and we have some work to do," Bernie said, and he wrapped big hairy his arm around my shoulder and escorted me and Sister Mary Subjugation out a side door in his office, where there was a small antechamber at whose opposite end stood what appeared to be a bank vault: a massive gray steel door with a combination lock and a chrome-plated flywheel used to open it, which was adorned with a solitary brass plate that read, "Department of Beatifications, Canonizations and Relics." Above us was a rail of out-of-place halogen track lights, the heat from which pounded on my head and made me feel like I was being interrogated.

Bernie dialed the combination, spun the chrome-plated flywheel to open the door, and motioned me to enter the massive room, filled as it was with score upon score of nuns and friars, diligently set to work. "So sensitive is this area that we lock the employees in during business hours," Bernie said as he swung the safe door open. Once safely inside with the door closed behind us, Bernie held out both of his arms, directing my gaze at the room. "This, Steve," he said, "is my soon-to-be-growing mini-empire, the Department of Beatifications, Canonizations and Relics. No one is allowed in here except upon order from this pope!"

"The pope wanted me here?"

"Yup."

"Wow!"

"He saw a live feed of your speech, and was impressed."

"The pope was impressed with me?"

"Absolutely," said Bernie. "Absolutely. And there's good news in it for you, too, Steve. You're being considered for canonization."

"Sainthood? Me?"

"Yup."

"But saints have to be dead, and I'm not dead."

"Yet," said Bernie, "but realistically you will be, and because anyone who gives his life for the Church is automatically considered a saint, you don't even need to be nominated or go through a hearing or anything. It's just, Wham! You're a saint!"

"Wham, you're a saint?"

"Right. If you give your life you're a martyr, and if you're a martyr you're automatically a saint. Wham!"

"Wham?"

"Wham! That's how much we value what you're doing for us, Steve: you'll get an automatic promotion to saint. And as soon as we get this Living Sainthood thing off the ground, assuming you're still among the Living...." Bernie nudged me.

"I'm a shoo-in?"

"You got it, boy," and he nudged me again.

I took a deep breath. "Thank you," I said. "But I'm just a translator!"

"Just a translator!" Bernie said. "Just a translator! If you only knew how important your work is to Bushistotle!" Bernie sat down on top of an empty desk, tapped on the one next to it motioning me to sit there, which I did. "And you're a real team player in that regard. But I get ahead of myself." He then stood atop the desk as if he were giving the Sermon on the Mount, opened his arms and spoke in a loud voice one notch below shouting: "All of this is mine, Steve. It's mine. Mine, mine, all mine!" There was muffled applause, and he sat down again. "Look over there, Steve." Bernie pointed at a far corner. "You see that cluster of metal desks?"

"Yes."

"That," Bernie said, "is another one of our task forces. Our second largest one, in fact, with over 50 members. It's the Pious XII canonization task force, code named 'Task Force PXII.' And you know what they're tasked with right now?"

"No."

"Quashing those nasty pro-Nazi rumors. Entirely untrue, entirely untrue. As if poor Cardinal Pacelli could have single-handedly stared Hitler down, or like have saved people. Nonsense, pure nonsense: he had his own ass to save, and lots of paintings and statues! And then this right here..."—Bernie banged on the empty desk he was sitting on, one of a cluster of three empty desks—"...this is the John XXIII canonization task force, code named 'Task Force J-No.' The current thinking here is that he was detrimental to the Church, far too nice a guy. Led to degeneration, a lack of discipline, so there's not a lot of effort being put in there."

"I see," I said.

Bernie then took me down a narrow space between rows of desks. "Right here," he said, "know what they're doing?"

I saw about a dozen nuns working furiously at computers. "No," I answered.

"Spamming for miracles," Bernie said. "You need two-plus miracles attributed to you to be declared a saint, so these dedicated ladies are spamming around the world, looking for people willing to claim for whatever reason—fame, fortune, an eBay auction, whatever—that they are the recipients of miracles by our candidates for sainthood, you know, through prayer or whatever. Most people claim to have been healed of cancer, and we'll accept that, but we're really looking for something spectacular. You know, newsworthy, like somebody falling out of an airplane from 40,000 feet and having a soft landing after kissing their ass good-bye and praying to Mother Teresa on the way down, or something. So far nothing like that, and we don't want to prompt. We want spontaneous, and we want to take people at their word, however farfetched that can be sometimes. And over there...." Bernie pointed to a cluster of about 20 desks some ten feet away. "Those nuns are doing research, weeding out all the answers we get back from Baptists. Seems that Baptists are performing miracles all the time, constantly healing people of this and that. We gotta make sure we don't inadvertently nominate a Baptist, which is a real cat-and-mouse game because they're always trying to trip us up."

"I see," I said.

Bernie then brought me to what looked like a display case with a loom in it. "Know what this is?" he asked.

"A loom?"

"Not just <u>a</u> loom," Bernie said. "<u>The</u> loom! That's the loom that we wove the Shroud of Turin on, one of our most effective publicity stunts ever. Water into wine is my second favorite, but damn, that Shroud thing is something you can <u>look at</u>! It's an image that really sticks with you, isn't it?"

"Uhm, yup."

"And over there?" Bernie pointed to a row of very old paper shredders.

"The shredders?"

"That's where we shredded the parts of the Dead Sea Scrolls we didn't like, the parts we didn't want to get out in public. You know, the parts that didn't fit into accepted doctrine. We call them the Apocrypha Shredders. They're the allegorical successor to bonfires."

"Nice."

"Yeah, I'm particularly proud of them because they don't pollute."

"I understand," I said.

Then Bernie pointed to a booth in the corner that looked much like my Isolation Booth, except it contained row after row of plasma HDTV's. "That over there, Steve, know what it is?"

"No."

"It's the Pro-Spin Zone, a private little P.R. project of mine that I'm doing on the side with a little of last year's leftover budget and a lot of hush-hush soft money from influential multinational let-us-call-them 'parishioners.' We monitor the news, and any time anybody says anything about one of our saints or candidates, bang! we send out a press release refuting it, quoting some of the best of the thousands and thousands of pages of documentation we have on why x, y, or z person is, was, or should be a saint. It's our Ready-Response solution to bad press, and we're building a database of Talking Points on each and every one of our saints and candidates, Bushistotle included. In fact, we have an extra big one for Bushistotle, had to buy a new server because there was so much to refute and deny. We want no more St. Christopher fiascos. Never again! How can we claim to be infallible when something like that brews up, snowballs out of control? No, never again. St. Patrick was close—you know, that 'never any snakes in Ireland' bullshit!—but we got control of that one right from the start, nipped it in the bud. But the St. Christopher thing, that's the whole Second Vatican Council problem, all J-No's fault."

"It is?"

"Steve, we had an entire industry set up minting St. Christopher medals, millions of adherents appealing to those medals for help and buying new ones when they tarnished, had to scuttle the whole shebang, promote St. Jude or whoever we promoted, cast new dyes, etc., etc., and so on and so forth. Okay there was a modest profit on the trade-ins and recycling, but it didn't outweigh the embarrassment, so you get the idea. Secular Humanism is what led to that, too much reliance on science rather than good ol' faith, which is why J-No's candidacy is hopeless for at least a thousand years. It's part of the slow death of the Left: they put way too much stock in reality, and that goddamned monkey-tainted evolution 'theory.' That's our next target— God's True Word is on our side, by the way, but we're letting the Evangelicals take the first hit since it means so much more to Literalists. Science is a slippery slope that we sure as hell don't want to start sliding down because the Word of God is so much more malleable."

Bernie then led Sister Mary Subjugation and me into a soundproof conference room that had several dozen squawk boxes laid out in an array on the table. "Now let's get down to business," Bernie said. "Our job here is to seek proof that saints lead exemplary lifestyles regardless of how hard we have to look to find that proof or invent it, and today we're working on Bushistotle again. Once we turn on the speaker phones, Steve, you'll be identified only by your code name: Agent 99."

"Agent 99?"

"Right now there are 100 members on Task Force B.S., and they're numbered sequentially. You're the second-to-last."

"Gotcha," I said.

"Now, here's where we are on this thing," Bernie said. "We've got volumes and volumes of documentation that supports the beatification of Bushistotle, as well as a few pieces that don't. The worst of the worst in the Don't Column we're just going to shred as apocryphal, but we don't want this thing to look like a slam-dunk even though it is, or like we're ramming it down the throats of Christendom, even though we are. By the way, if anybody ever asks, the official line here is that Christendom means Catholics, and perhaps someday Lutherans and Episcopalians if our ecumenical talks go better in the future and they realize how wrong they've been for the past few hundred years, and repent."

"Is that likely?" I asked.

"There's always a chance, and it'd be a lot better for their dead ancestors salvation-wise, if you know what I mean. Anyhow, let's get down to business; you're the last person I have to brief before we move onto our conference call. Sister Naomi has been rummaging through the Secret Archives as usual, finding what she can to support our case while she dusts. The whole Windex thing was a freak accident, and now we've limited her to a feather duster, so we shouldn't run into that problem again."

"Thank God for that," I said. "The ammonia reeks and can really get to you sometimes."

Sister Mary Subjugation wrinkled her brow and held her nose à la "P-U."

"Agreed, and sorry about that Stevie," Bernie said. "Ditto, Sister. Anyhow, just yesterday she happened upon a very important document: Bushistotle's genealogy."

"It was in the Secret Archives?"

Bernie looked at Sister Mary Subjugation before answering, who looked down at the table. Then he said, "It was, and it's very important. It clearly shows what this pope knew all along: that Bushistotle was related to Jesus."

Bushistotle was related to Jesus? Now that was a shock to me! "Jesus who?" I asked, just to make sure.

"The one and only."

"The one and only?"

"Jesus Christ."

"Really?"

"Yes. The fact of the matter is, Steve, at least according to our new information, Jesus wasn't descended from the House of David at all, but rather from the House of Bushistotle."

"The House of Bushistotle?"

"A true dynasty it was, too!" Bernie exclaimed. "It occurred on account of Bushistotle's campaign against the Persians. Seems that like King David himself Bushistotle sowed his wild oats a little too wildly all throughout the Middle East...."

"Like Jesus and Mary Magdalene?"

"That's very Gnostic of you Steve and I really do wish you'd quit it," Bernie said, "but our information from the historical record is that he screwed everybody he could in that part of the world, which might be how the confusion arose. It presents us with a big problem, though..."

"I guess it does!"

"...and that's where you come in. You see, Steve, Sister Naomi found two different accounts of Bushistotle's genealogy, and we don't think they're the same. But one's written in Greek and the other's written in Aramaic, and we've got to compare and contrast the two and either decide which one we keep and which one we run through the Apocrypha Shredders, or come up with a compelling reason why the two versions are different, like maybe one's was his mom's side the other's was his dad's." Bernie took an ancient parchment sheet out of a steel Halliburton briefcase that was lying on the table, set it before me. "This is the Greek one, Steve. Do you feel comfortable doing a little sight-translation of it for us?"

"W-, w-, w-, w-ell," I stuttered, "I, I, I didn't bring my dictionary along."

"No matter for now," Bernie said. "We just want a general idea of the names involved; we'll get you to working on the detailed translation later. You ready?"

I looked at the parchment folio: it was difficult to read and looked authentic enough, but I was not convinced. "How is it possible that so many millennia have passed without anyone finding this information before?" I asked Bernie.

"Before Sister Naomi the Archives were a real mess."

"But still, she's been alive for thousands of years...."

"Well, if we're right, it might be the reason why all the predictions for Jesus' imminent return haven't come true: we've been working with the wrong version of the Holy Scripture! We're working on that now, too."

"I see," I said.

"I'm turning on the squawk box, let's hope there's no feedback," Bernie said. "You'll be talking to Agent 33, who is the Aramaic translator assigned to this job."

"Agent 33?"

"Right. He was involved with the Mel Gibson movie, which is how we found him: great references!" Bernie switched on the squawk box. "Agent 33? Come in, Agent 33. Are you there?"

"Here, Bernie," announced a high-pitched fey voice over the squawk box.

"I have Agent 99 here."

"Nice to meet you, 99," said Agent 33.

"Likewise, 33," I answered.

"Okay, boys, you know the rules. No fraternizing allowed until we go public with this thing: right now it's still a Top Secret Project!"

"Gotcha," Agent 33 and I said simultaneously.

"Now, Steve, go ahead and start reading your text."

"Okay," I said. I struggled a bit with the faded letters but after a moment I figured it out: "The book of the generation of Jesus Christ, the son of BUSHISTOTLE, the son of Abraham...."

"Okay, stop!" shouted Agent 33 over the squawk box. "99, I have a whole bunch of names here that connect Bushistotle right back to God. Let me run through them, see if you can find any in your text: God...."

I scanned. "Nope."
"Adam."
"Nope."
"Seth."
"Nope."
"Enosh."
"Nope."
"Kenan."
"Nope."
"Mahalalel."
"Nope."
"Jared."
"Nope."
"Enoch."
"Nope."
"Methuselah."
"Nope."
"Lamech."
"Nope."
"Noah."
"Nope."
"Shem."
"Nope."
"Arphaxad."
"Nope."
"Cainan."
"Nope."
"Shelah."
"Nope."
"Eber."
"Nope."
"Peleg."
"Nope."

"Reu."
"Nope."
"Serug."
"Nope."
"Nahor."
"Nope."
"Terah."
"Nope."
"Abraham."
"HIT!" I shouted.
"Hmmm," Bernie said. "Steve, I mean Agent 99, your list doesn't seem to have a direct route from Bushistotle back to God."
"Not that I can see, but I can keep on looking."
"We'll leave that for the detailed translation later," Bernie said. "What do you have next?"
"Abraham begat Isaac," I answered.
"Hit!" shouted Agent 33.
"Excellent!" said Bernie.
"Isaac begat Jacob."
"Hit!"
"And Jacob begat Judas and his brethren."
"Hit!"
"And Judas begat Phares and Zara of Thamar."
"Hit!"
"And Phares begat Esrom."
"Hit!"
"And Esrom begat Aram."
"Hit!"
"And Aram begat Aminadab."
"Hit!"
"And Aminadab begat Naasson."
"Hit!"
"And Naasson begat Salmon."
"Hit!"
"And Salmon begat Booz of Rachab."
"Hit!"
"And Booz begat Obed of Ruth."
"Hit!"
"And Obed begat Jesse."

"Hit!"

"And Jesse begat BUSHISTOTLE the Philosopher-Warrior-King."

"HIT!" shouted Agent 33.

"Excellent, boys, excellent!" Bernie proclaimed. "At least we can agree that there's a direct link between Bushistotle and Abraham, and since we know Abraham is directly descended from God through Adam we're on fairly strong firmament here, so to speak. What do you have next, Steve?"

"And BUSHISTOTLE the Philosopher-Warrior-King begat Solomon of Karen, who was the Oracle at Delphi," I said.

I stopped dead in my tracks. *Oh, my God*, I thought. *Maybe "The Temptation of Bushistotle" isn't apocryphal after all! Maybe it is for real!* But of course I couldn't say anything at the time, because I didn't want anyone to know that it was in my possession.

"Hit!" said Agent 33.

"And Solomon begat Roboam."

"Miss!"

"And Roboam begat Abia."

"Miss!"

"And Abia begat Asa."

"Miss!"

"And Asa begat Josaphat."

"Miss!"

"And Josaphat begat Joram."

"Miss!"

"And Joram begat Ozias."

"Miss!"

"And Ozias begat Joatham."

"Miss!"

"And Joatham begat Achaz."

"Miss!"

"And Achaz begat Ezekias."

"Miss!"

"And Ezekias begat Manasses."

"Miss!"

"And Manasses begat Amon."

"Miss!"

"And Amon begat Josias."

"Miss!"

"And Josias begat Jechonias and his brethren, about the time they were carried away to Babylon."

"Miss!"

"And after they were brought to Babylon, Jechonias begat Salathiel."

"Hit!" cried Agent 33.

"Excellent!" said Bernie. "It's about time!"

"And Salathiel begat Zorobabel."

"Hit!"

"Excellent again!" said Bernie.

"And Zorobabel begat Abiud."

"Miss!"

"Damn!" shouted Bernie. "I thought we were on a roll, there, too!"

"And Abiud begat Eliakim."

"Hit!"

"Excellent!" said Bernie. "Right back on track!"

"Hey, but wait a minute Bernie," Agent 33 said. "My Eliakim comes 1, 2, 3, 4, 5, 6, 7, 8, 9, 10, 11, 12, 13, 14, 15, 16 generations earlier than 99's Eliakim, so maybe it's not the same Eliakim?"

"Maybe my Eliakim is Eliakim Jr., Jr., Jr., Jr., Jr., Jr., Jr., Jr., Jr., Jr., Jr., Jr., Jr., Jr., Jr.," I said, counting on my fingers, "and 33's Eliakim is Eliakim Sr., Sr., Sr., Sr., Sr., Sr., Sr., Sr., Sr., Sr., Sr., Sr., Sr., Sr., Sr.," also counting on my fingers.

I thought I saw another Mona Lisa smile on Sister Mary Subjugation's face, but perhaps not.

"No funny business Steve, I mean Agent 99," Bernie said. "We are not to make fun of the Word of God, however inconsistent it is."

"Understood," I said.

"Good! Now let's continue."

"And Eliakim begat Azor," I said.

"Miss!" said Agent 33.

"And Azor begat Sadoc."

"Miss!"

"And Sadoc begat Achim."

"Miss!"

"And Achim begat Eliud."

"Miss!"

"And Eliud begat Eleazar."

"Miss!"

"And Eleazar begat Matthan."

"Miss!"

"And Matthan begat Jacob."

"Miss!"

"And Jacob begat Joseph the husband of Mary, of whom was born Jesus, who is called Christ," I said.

"At last, another hit!" cried Agent 33.

"And that brings us right to Jesus," Bernie said, "which is what Task Force B.S. is all about. But I'm not liking the looks of some of this boys, and Sister, because we don't have it absolutely, 100% proved that Bushistotle is descended directly from God."

"Aren't we all?" asked Agent 33.

"In a sense, Tom—I mean Agent 33—yes," Bernie explained, "but not through Abraham and Isaac we're not, and that's what we were looking for. And then there are these huge discrepancies between the texts regarding exactly how Bushistotle begat Jesus and through how many generations, and we're going to have to resolve that, too. I think, Agents 33 and 99, and Sister, that we're going to put this part of the project on hold for a while, at least until I've had the chance to talk to this pope about it, come up with a new strategy."

"But I have some more text here," I protested.

"And I have dozens of names here that haven't even been mentioned," Agent 33 said.

"Thanks guys, but this part of the Bushistotle Beatification Project is on hold for right now. And of course remember that you're not allowed to discuss it with anyone. If this genealogy mess leaks out and people find out how much trouble we're actually having linking Bushistotle forward to Jesus and backward again to God, then our project will go right down the drain along with my career, for the second time."

"Understood," Agent 33 and I said in unison. And of course there was nothing to worry about regarding Sister Mary Subjugation, since she couldn't talk to anybody about anything, anyway.

So Bushistotle was related to Jesus and Jesus was related to Bushistotle! Any way you slice it it was bound to be some of the most important new information about our Lord to have come out of Rome in centuries. But would it also mean that the Bushistotle Doctrine of Preemptive Retaliation was actually blessed by God? Or that the Bushistotle Ideal of "One Nation under the Gods" was truly divine in origin, even though, historically at least, Bushistotle did not share the same God as the Vatican, or the Persians, or as most other people in the world? And if this were so, how could all of this be squared with "Truth, Goodness, and the Athenian Way?"

I did not have immediate answers to these pressing questions, and though I had heard of kings declaring themselves descendants of Jesus before, most notably the Merovingians, I a) didn't believe it, and b) had never in any case heard of anyone doing it the other way around, that is, challenging the genealogy of Christ, claiming that he was descended not from King David but from another king, in this case Bushistotle, the great Philosopher-Warrior one of Athens, or any other one for that matter, or just descended from regular people, you know, good old peasant stock like you and me. Yet that is clearly what the rest of the document I had been given to sight-translate said:

So all the generations from Abraham to BUSHISTOTLE are fourteen generations; and from BUSHISTOTLE until the carrying away into Babylon are fourteen generations; and from the carrying away into Babylon unto Christ are fourteen generations. Now the birth of Jesus Christ was on this wise: When as his mother Mary was espoused to Joseph, before they came together, she was found with child of the Holy Ghost. Then Joseph her husband, being a just man, and not willing to make her a public example, was minded to put her away privily. But while he thought on these things, behold, the angel of the Lord appeared unto him in a dream, saying, Joseph, thou son of BUSHISTOTLE, fear not to take unto thee Mary thy wife: for that which is conceived in her is of the Holy Ghost. And she shall bring forth a son, and thou shalt call his name Jesus: for he shall save his people from their sins. Now all this was done, that it might be fulfilled which was spoken of the Lord by the prophet, saying: Behold, a virgin shall be with child, and shall bring forth a son, and they shall call his name Emmanuel, which being interpreted is, God with us. Then Joseph being raised from sleep did as the angel of the Lord had bidden him, and took unto him his wife: And knew her not till she had brought forth her firstborn son: and he called his name Jesus.

I never found out what the full text of Agent 33's Aramaic document said, so I don't know to what extent it might corroborate what I had learned: the Vatican was very adept at keeping members of Task Force B.S. apart, and only Bernie seemed to know who we all were. Yet what I thought I had read in that text was very clear inasmuch as it confirmed that Bushistotle, the Philosopher-Warrior-King of Athens, "begat Solomon of Karen, who was the Oracle at Delphi," exactly what "The Temptation of Bushistotle" implied was possible by documenting his extramarital affair. Of course my ancient Greek sucks—or at best is nonexistent—so nothing of what I sight-translated may actually have been written on that page, but the chances of two such coincidental misreadings are in my estimation very low indeed.

But would Bushistotle—apparently a man of impeccable character, or so he claimed—actually screw an oracle and cheat on Mrs. Bushistotle, the love of his life? Certainly there was no indication of this in Carolus Rovus' <u>The Life and Times of Bushistotle</u> that I recalled, but it had been years since I'd read that work, and even then it was on the heels of <u>Profiles in Courage</u>, which made it pale in comparison. Perhaps the answer would lie in a later chapter of <u>Dudley the Donkey Learns a Lesson</u>, but that I could only find out if I translated more of the text. If it is true, however, it is no wonder that King Solomon was so wise and prescient a ruler as to decide that the best way to ascertain maternity is by cutting the baby in half: he was the offspring of Bushistotle and Karen, the famed Oracle at Delphi!

Since the St. Bushistotle Genealogy Project was temporarily on hold until Bernie could pow-wow with the pope to figure a way out of the contradictory-text pickle that he found himself in, with Sister Mary Subjugation seated next to me as usual I continued to work on the next installment of my translation in the Secret Archives' Isolation Booth that had become my home-away-from-home. Call it an accident of timing or whatever, but this part of the history I was given to translate seemed entirely favorable to Bushistotle, so the original text required hardly any redacting at all:

The Bushistotle Campaign against Byzantium was going well: who would have ever thunk that Athens would declare war against Persia in retaliation for Sparta's attack on Syracuse? No one, which is why it was such a brilliant surprise, and why Persia was caught off-guard!

Now that the Athenian army had entered Byzantium so the coast was clear and they were out of harm's way, the ruling Bushistotle Coterie was meeting poopside on the Athenian Navy's flagship, the S.S. Bushistotle, moored in the port of Piraeus on the outskirts of Athens, ready to set sail for Byzantium, where Bushistotle would take his rightful place as ruler. Atop the ship flew a banner reading, "Mission Accomplished: Thank You, Bushistotle!"; Mrs. Bushistotle had hand-embroidered it herself in homage to her Philosopher-Warrior-King husband.

Stretching in his chaise longue and sipping on a frozen margarita, Cheneyon offered a toast to Bushistotle: "Based on your visionary leadership and hard work in spreading the Athenian Ideals of 'One Nation under the Gods' and 'Truth, Goodness, and the Athenian Way,' I toast you, Honorable Bushistotle!"

"Aw, shucks!" Bushistotle said. "It was nothing, really!"

"I second that toast," cried Constantina. "Here's to war!"

"HAIL BUSHISTOTLE!" cried the Plenary Coterie, and they toasted to Bushistotle's greatness.

"Furthermore," said Cheneyon, "based on these principles, I move that we begin the job of drafting the Constitution of the New Republic. Do I have a second?"

"What are we agreeing to?" asked Bushistotle.

"To making you the King of Kings," answered Cheneyon.

"I second that!" said Bushistotle.

"All in favor?" asked Cheneyon.

The Coterie shouted, "Aye!"

"All against?" asked Cheneyon, and there was silence.

"It is done!" said Cheneyon. "It is done!"

"Now it is time to begin our work silencing activist left-wing judges," said Ashcroftus, "and to institute a city-state in the image of Bushistotle himself!"

"You mean all for me and me for all," asked Bushistotle, "and then maybe some leftovers for my friends?"

"Exactly," said Powellonius. "And as part of this we must undertake programs that will foster responsible fatherhood, for these will have long-lasting benefits for families and for communities!"

"Amen to that!" said Constantina. "Amen to that!"

Then a female voice shouted from the dock: "Bushy! Bushy! You forgot this!"

It was Karen, the Oracle at Delphi, laden with child and waving Bushistotle's copy of <u>Dudley the Donkey Learns a Lesson</u>, which in the heat of passion he had dropped on the belly-button of the world.

Another reference to Karen the Oracle! I thought as I translated this segment. *So "The Temptation of Bushistotle" wasn't apocryphal at all!* But since I could not let on what I knew to Sister Mary Subjugation I returned to translating the text: *"You dropped this, Bushy! You dropped this!" Karen the Oracle shouted.*

Rumsfeldiavelli turned to Bushistotle. "Honorable Bushistotle," he said, "who is that crazed woman?"

"Karen," Bushistotle answered, "the Oracle at Delphi. She's been stalking me ever since I went up to the omphalus to get her prediction about what would happen with the invasion. I accidentally left my copy of <u>Dudley the Donkey Learns a Lesson</u> there, but I'm afraid to ask for it back because I don't want to encourage her."

"Shall I have our archers take care of her?" Rumsfeldiavelli asked.

"No," said Bushistotle. "I learned the hard way: never fuck with an oracle."

"Understood, sir."

"You know," Bushistotle lamented, "I really don't know what her problem is. I set her up with her own small apartment at the Ακαδημια but she seems to want something more, like commitment...."

Here I stopped: I didn't recognize the word "Ακαδημια"—but really, who would?—and I couldn't find it in my pocket ancient Greek / modern American dictionary because that page was so heavily worn. Sister Mary Subjugation was dozing in the uncomfortable chair behind me; I thought to wake her and ask if I could ask a libarian to help me find a better dictionary, but I recalled my previous pithy admonition to myself that waking her would be akin to tapping a porcupine on the shoulder and asking him to get out of my driveway, so I thought it best to wait till she woke up in her own good time.

I slouched back in my own uncomfortable chair and suddenly felt overwhelmed with emotion: perhaps it was the sheer beauty of the Bushistotle story that was moving me to tears, or the frustration of not knowing what Ακαδημια meant when I'd obviously looked it up a thousand times before, but more likely it was that I hadn't had contact with my family or my friends or my cats for I don't know how long, and I wasn't even sure my rent was being paid. And what's worse, it seemed like I would never get to take that longish weekend vacation on the coast of southern France that I deep-down longed for: there was a much greater likelihood that I wouldn't make it out of the Vatican alive than there was of their awarding me an all-expenses-paid weekend getaway to the French Riviera for my efforts: although they almost always live in luxury, clerics prefer that their faithful live more modestly.

I heaved a heavy sigh and closed my eyes and tears formed in their corners: I was completely isolated from the world! Then, out of the blue, I felt a long and crooked index finger stroking my hand: Sister Mary Subjugation was going to zap me! But no, this time I was wrong; Sister Mary Subjugation's intention seemed to be to try to console me. So touched was I that I could control myself no longer, and I began to sob aloud; Sister Mary Subjugation held me tight in her arms.

I recovered after a few minutes, but found it difficult to speak. "I guess I got upset because I don't know what Ακαδημια means," I forced out, then I sort of laughed, and sniffled. "Can I ask a libarian to help me find a better dictionary, please?"

Sister Mary Subjugation looked at me and seemed to be thinking *not looking like that you can't!*, so instead of releasing me into the libary she took the keyboard and mouse, clicked on the Start button, hit "Log Off Steven," then "Switch Users," where I saw another userid: Penelope.

That cheered me right up! "Sister Penelope?" I asked.

She shook her head yes, logged on, and went to Google, where I typed in Ακαδημια. Bingo, a dozen websites came up which gave me the proper translation: "Academy and/or Bushistotle Center."

"Thank you, sister," I said. "I don't know how I forgot that word!"

She nodded, took the keyboard and mouse back and went to Hotmail, where she clicked on "New Message," and handed me the keyboard. "I can send an email?" I asked.

She held up her long and crooked index finger: one.

One would be enough, I thought, if only I could type "Help! I'm locked in a fortune cookie factory" or something Catholically analogous like "Help! The convent doors are locked!" but I didn't even try: I was certain that Sister Mary Subjugation—I mean Sister

Penelope, as was her real name—wouldn't let me send it despite today's uncharacteristic onslaught of compassion; the penalty for trying could be death. So I just wrote: "Dear Mom: Hope the cats are well. Please pay my rent. I'll be home soon. Love, Me." The "Love" part was pretty mawkish considering that the message was only for my mother, but I always signed my emails "me" so this way she'd know it was me.

"Thank you, Sister," I said.

She nodded and logged me back on; silently I made plans to hack into her userid at a later date, but what password might a nun use? "Paraclete" was my first guess, because no one would ever figure it out. Otherwise, "homoousion" would be good, as would "Septuagint," because nobody would guess those too fast, either. I could have come up with others, as well, but every move I made was being watched by Sister Penelope, so I returned to my translation work: *"I don't know where women get ideas like that," said Rumsfeldiavelli. "You know, commitment."*

"No," added Ashcroftus.

Constantina cleared her throat impatiently. "Can we just set sail?" she asked, interrupting the male bonding that was going on around her.

"Yes," said Powellonius. "We don't want the Oracle causing a scene."

"Bad P.R.," Cheneyon concurred.

"Agreed, Number One," said Bushistotle.

"Weigh anchor!" shouted Rumsfeldiavelli, and on that command the S.S. Bushistotle set sail for Byzantium, with the forlorn figure of Karen the Oracle at Delphi growing ever smaller on the distant dock, and her voice—"You dropped this, Bushy! Bushy, you dropped this!"—growing fainter and fainter till it was gone.

The seas were calm for the S.S. Bushistotle's maiden voyage, and the breeze was light and favorable. Frozen margaritas, tortilla chips and salsa abounded for Bushistotle and his Coterie to snack on, though the shiphands and oarsmen were sweating their balls off to make sure the boat got to Persia on time. To the dismay of Constantina and not a few other Coterie members, Ashcroftus took off his shirt to catch a few rays, but since he was in charge of "interviewing" Persian prisoners at the penal colony on Patmos, no one put up a fuss.

The "Mission Accomplished: Thank You, Bushistotle!" banner waived proudly in the air atop the S.S. Bushistotle's mizzenmast, temporarily blocking Rumsfeldiavelli's sun. He got up and changed chaises, and ordered a new frozen margarita since his ice had already melted.

Sitting in the shade so as not to get too much more color, Constantina took out her signed copy of <u>Dudley the Donkey Learns a Lesson</u>, and began to read to herself. Moments later, Bushistotle saw her. "Honorable Constantina," he said. "Can I have your copy of <u>Dudley</u>? Mrs. Bushistotle is mighty sore that I lost mine!"

"Honorable Bushistotle, you that know I am loyal," said Constantina, "but giving up my copy of <u>Dudley</u>!?"

"It means a lot to me," said Bushistotle.

"But Mrs. Bushistotle signed it for me," Constantina said, holding up the title page. "She wrote, 'Thank you, Consti, for being so loyal to the Bushistotles. Love, Mrs. Bushistotle.' So she'd know it wasn't your copy!"

"I see," said Bushistotle sadly. Then he asked whether any of the other members of the Coterie had a copy of <u>Dudley</u> that he could have.

"Nope," said Powellonius.

"Sorry," said Cheneyon.

"Don't," said Rumsfeldiavelli.

"I do," said Ashcroftus, "but I left it back in Athens."

"Gosh, darn it!" exclaimed Bushistotle. "I really do miss the wisdom of <u>Dudley</u>!"

"We all do," said Cheneyon. "We all do."

"Then why don't I read aloud?" suggested Constantina. "To enlighten us all!"

"Oh, yes!" said Ashcroftus. "Please do!"

"Yes, indeed!" cried Bushistotle.

But the rest of the Coterie merely groaned, and Powellonius ordered another drink.

"Where did we leave off?" asked Constantina.

"The Honorable Bushistotle was explaining 'binarialism,'" answered Ashcroftus, "which is one of my favorite parts."

"Well my favorite part comes up next," said Constantina, "because it explains the effect of 'binarialism' on foreign policy."

"The Bushistotle Doctrine...," said Bushistotle proudly.

"...of Preemptive Retaliation," added Cheneyon. "Truly brilliant!"

Then Constantina began to read aloud: "'The warm dry winds of the Macedonian Outback began to blow strong, and Bushistotle, the Philosopher-Warrior-King of Athens, suggested that it might be a good idea for them to go inside.'"

"It can get mighty hot in Macedonia in the summer," Bushistotle said. All agreed with him.

The waiter brought Powellonius' third frozen margarita; everyone noticed that he had too much to drink that day, but no one said anything to him.

Constantina continued. "'Once inside, Mrs. Bushistotle served Dudley and her husband Bushistotle, the Philosopher-Warrior-King of Athens, some freshly baked shoofly pie. Dudley, of course, having hoofs instead of hands, was forced to eat the pie right out of the pie pan with his face, but Mrs. Bushistotle thought that that was better than eating out of the Bushistotles' garbage.

""'Maybe if we fed him more he wouldn't eat our garbage," Mrs. Bushistotle suggested to Bushistotle, the Philosopher-Warrior-King of Athens.

""'Oh, Mrs. Bushistotle," said Bushistotle, the Philosopher-Warrior-King of Athens, "that is so silly. Why, I fed him last just two days ago! You wouldn't want him to eat too much, would you, because what good is having a fat ass?"

"'Dudley finished the shoofly pie and brayed, "Hee-haw."

""'I think now that our stomachs are full of shoofly pie we're ready for our next lesson," Mrs. Bushistotle said to her husband Bushistotle, the Philosopher-Warrior-King of Athens.

""'Very well," said Bushistotle, the Philosopher-Warrior-King of Athens. "The next lesson is on how to be good neighbors."''

"This lesson is based on the events of September 11, 350 BC, when the Spartans attacked us so we were forced to declare war on Persia," Bushistotle said to his Coterie.

Constantina read, "'Dudley the Donkey brayed in bemusement.

""'But Dudley," said Bushistotle, the Philosopher-Warrior-King of Athens, "you, the other asses and I discussed how to be good neighbors, and we were in full agreement at the time."

"'Dudley the Donkey brayed in bemusement.'"

"Mrs. Bushistotle sure does like that word, doesn't she, Honorable Bushistotle?" asked Constantina.

"Yes she does," answered Bushistotle, his mouth full of tortilla chips. "I told her not to use it because it will alienate our readers, but she insists."

"I think it takes away from some of the essential message," said Cheneyon, "which is that because of you, Honorable Bushistotle, our city-state is more secure. Because of you, the tyrant has fallen, and Persia is free."

"What tyrant has fallen?" Bushistotle asked.

"Saladin," answered Cheneyon.

"Saladin who?" asked Bushistotle

"The tyrant of Persia," answered Cheneyon. "Didn't you know?"

"No one told me!"

"I'm pretty sure it was in a briefing," Rumsfeldiavelli said.

"I don't remember that briefing," Bushistotle said.

"I'm pretty sure we had a briefing," Cheneyon said. He nudged Bushistotle with his elbow.

Bushistotle turned toward him. "Ouch! What do you mean, 'pretty sure?'"

"Pretty sure, because that's why we're on this boat."

"Is that why we're on this boat?" asked Bushistotle. "I was wondering what we were doing here, what all this 'Mission Accomplished' crap was."

"We're sailing to Byzantium, so you can sit in judgment of Saladin, and claim your rightful place as emperor!"

"How did it happen?" asked Bushistotle. "How did Saladin fall?"

"He was captured in a hole," answered Rumsfeldiavelli.

"Really?" said Bushistotle. "What was he doing in a hole?"

"He was hiding," said Rumsfeldiavelli. "He was afraid of you."

"What a scaredy-cat!" Bushistotle said. "Afraid of little ol' me!"

"He told our Special Operations Forces that you were unstable," said Powellonius.

"Which is what makes you such a fearsome leader," said Constantina. "Nobody ever knows what you're liable to do next!"

"We didn't torture him to get that information, I promise," said Ashcroftus.

"And I believe you," said Bushistotle. "I believe you."

"When we arrive at Byzantium, you are to sit in judgment of him," said Rumsfeldiavelli. "And once you find him guilty, you will assume your rightful place as emperor!"

"Well you know," Bushistotle said, "when I was governor of Macedonia, I signed 152 death warrants. So what's 153?"

"Your lucky number!" said Ashcroftus.

The Plenary Coterie laughed together aloud: it was the first bonding-moment they had shared in a long time.

"Now we can claim this as a glorious victory, can we not?" asked Bushistotle.

"Hear, hear!" said Powellonius. "A glorious victory!"

"Hear, hear!" shouted the Plenary Coterie. "Hear, hear!"

The Plenary Coterie raised their frozen margarita glasses and toasted to Bushistotle's good health.

"Where is Carolus Rovus to spin this the right way?" asked Bushistotle, smacking his lips. "You know, to show the world how we're doing justice and spreading democracy by hanging the evildoers from the nearest tree?"

"He gets seasick," said Rumsfeldiavelli, "but I advise caution: new leaders are rising up."

"But we are crushing them," said Cheneyon.

"At least we can now claim that major combat operations in Persia have ended," said Bushistotle. "In the Battle of Persia, Athens and our ally have prevailed! And now our coalition of one-plus-almost-none is engaged in securing and reconstructing that country."

"What ally are you talking about?" asked Powellonius.

"That soldier from Turkmenistan," said Rumsfeldiavelli, "who does guard duty, and I think somebody is on his way over from Guam, swimming."

"And the Trojans lent us a box of condoms," said Cheneyon. "Even though we're against sex outside of marriage, we know that rape, plunder, and pillage are a necessary part of war."

"Yes indeed they are," added Ashcroftus. "They're vital to getting information from the enemy."

"I wish I had known this before," Bushistotle said, "because now that Saladin is captured we can claim that in this battle, we have fought for the cause of liberty, and for the peace of the world. Our city-state and our coalition are proud of this accomplishment!"

"'Dudley the Donkey brayed in bemusement again,' Constantina then read from <u>Dudley</u>.

"'"But Dudley," said Bushistotle, the Philosopher-Warrior-King of Athens. "Any person, organization, or government that supports, protects, or harbors our enemies is complicit in the murder of the innocent, and equally guilty of crimes, even if they committed no crimes against us. Or in your mind are they not?"

"'Dudley the Donkey brayed in bemusement again.'"

"Well," Bushistotle told his Coterie, "I still think the Persians were complicit, even if there is no evidence to support me! We can't be soft on Spartans!"

Constantina read aloud again from <u>Dudley</u>: "'"Any regime except our own and those we like that possesses Weapons of <u>Mass</u> Destruction is a grave danger to the civilized world, and will be confronted," taught Bushistotle,

the Philosopher-Warrior-King of Athens, "unless they're too big for us, like China. This is the Bushistotle Doctrine of Preemptive Retaliation.""

Powellonius, somewhat tipsy by now, repeated what Constantina had just said: "Dudley the Donkey brayed in bemusement again."

"We have begun the search for hidden chemical and biological weapons, and already know of hundreds of sites that will be investigated, though nothing will be found," Bushistotle said to his Coterie.

"What?" asked Cheneyon.

"Nothing will be found," Bushistotle repeated. "It's what Karen told me, but I refuse to believe it."

The S.S. Bushistotle continued on its voyage, I continued translating, then I heard snoring and turned around: Sister Penelope had fallen asleep again, and who could blame her?

there is a vast right-wing conspiracy underway here in the Vatican to change all of recorded history."

"By making Bushistotle a saint?" I repeated.

"It's far worse than that, Steve," Bruno answered. "Can I count on your help in our Anti-Task Force B.S. operations?"

I wasn't fully convinced, but was willing to give it a try since I had no other option. "Can you help me escape?" I asked.

Bruno nodded. "Come with me," he then said, and he pushed a rolling bookshelf to one side, which revealed a secret passageway. I must have looked surprised, because Bruno said, "Not to worry, Steve. The Vatican is full of secret passageways. Otherwise, how could there be so many conspiracies here?"

Bruno flicked on the lights, closed the bookshelf behind us, and we entered into a long, low, dank concrete tunnel that rather reminded me of the photos I had seen of Hitler's Berlin bunker. Water dripped through the ceiling at places, and stalactites formed from there down as stalagmites rose to meet them. The lights were naked bulbs strung along an orange extension cord, which itself was hung on hooks. Half the bulbs had burnt out, and occasionally some had shattered, leaving thin shards of frosted glass on the concrete walkway. We had to crouch to fit through, and since it's really hard to talk while walking crouched because you have to concentrate on where you're going so as not to hit your head, there was no noise except the sound of my shoes and Bruno's Jerusalem sandals. We walked in single file, which meant that Bruno's fat ass was wagging in my face; honestly, I'd had better views in my life, including the non-view from my pre-upgrade cell.

After some five minutes that felt like five days, we arrived at the end of the tunnel. There was a small room there, and we were able to stand, or to sit on the concrete benches affixed to the concrete walls. There was a small opening in one of the walls at about eye level, which was covered by a locked wooden door. It felt good to stretch my back a bit.

"This is how we do it," Bruno said between huffs and puffs: a guy his size doesn't fit through tunnels easily.

"Do what?" I asked.

"Smuggle our texts in and out, and communicate with each other."

"Who?"

Decades of lies and disinformation could not make the Athenian people love Bushistotle their oppressor, or desire their own enslavement, read the introduction to the subsequent chapter of the ancient text, *and unrest was brewing among the people.* For my part I turned around again, and Sister Penelope was still asleep. I watched her closely, was certain that her sleep was sound, and I was just about to try to hack into her userid and send an emergency email for help—what was her password: "Paraclete," "homoousion," or "Septuagint"?—when there was a tap on the fishbowl window. It was Fra Diavolo, and he was winking at me. *Damn!* I thought. *I've managed to avoid the Reference Desk thus far, but now I'm gonna have to break the bad news to him: I don't do the tonsured look!*

Fra Diavolo motioned me to exit. I pointed furiously at Sister Penelope, but he tilted his head, pressed his palms together and placed them by his ear in a gesture of sleep, then motioned me to exit again. I stood up slowly making sure not to scratch the legs of my uncomfortable wooden chair against the floor, then I turned the knob and was out.

I was free! Free at last, free at last! Thank God Almighty, I was free at last!

Or at least out of the Isolation Booth.

Fra Diavolo motioned again, this time to remain quiet, and he escorted me down a long hall and then into dimly lit stacks of books. "Your name is Steve, right?" he asked.

"Yes."

"I'm Brother Bruno Giordano. But you can call me Bruno. All the boys do."

"Nice to meet you, Bruno."

We shook hands. "Oh, Steve," he said. "I need to confide in you."

Please don't, I thought, but instead I said, "In me?"

"We need allies. Can I trust you?"

I looked at him, and he looked sincere, and plaintive. "Allies in what?"

"Task Force B.S. is involved in the most insidious of plots!"

"Making Bushistotle a saint?"

"Cardinal Lei has no idea. In fact, he's pretty much an idiot, but

"Those of us who are trying to stop this rewriting of history." Bruno opened the small wooden door, which revealed a sort of safe. "There's another tunnel on the other side of this wall," Bruno said, "but you can't go from one to the other. The only connection is this small opening, which is where we leave things for each other."

"Who's we?"

"I don't know who the person or people on the other side is or are, and they don't know who I am. This way, if any of us is caught, we can't reveal each others' name."

Bruno took a piece of paper out of the safe, closed the wooden door. He read the text silently, then burst into anger: "Blasphemy! Pure blasphemy!"

He handed me the paper, and I read it:

"Men, brethren, and fathers," said Bushistotle. "Hear ye my defence which I make now unto you. I am verily a man taught according to the perfect manner of the law of the fathers, and was zealous toward our gods, as ye all are this day. And I persecuted this way unto the death, binding and delivering into prisons both men and women. As also the high priest doth bear me witness, and all the estate of the elders: from whom also I received letters unto the brethren, and went to Persia, to bring them which were there bound unto Patmos, for to be punished. And it came to pass, that, as I made my journey, and was come nigh unto Byzantium about noon, suddenly there shone from heaven a great light round about me. And I fell unto the ground, and heard a voice saying unto me, 'Bushistotle, Bushistotle, why persecutest thou me?' And I answered, 'Who art thou, Lord?' And he said unto me, 'I am the True God, whom thou persecutest through your false ones.' And they that were with me saw indeed the light, and were afraid; but they heard not the voice of him that spake to me. And I said, 'What shall I do, Lord?' And the Lord said unto me, 'Arise, and go unto Byzantium; and there it shall be told thee of all things which are appointed for thee to do.' And when I could not see for the glory of that light, being led by the hand of them that were with me, I came into Byzantium. And one Ananias, a devout man according to the law, having a good report of all those which dwelt there, came unto me, and stood, and said unto me, 'Brother Bushistotle, receive thy sight.' And the same hour I looked up upon him and he said: 'The God of our fathers hath chosen thee, that thou shouldest know his will, and see him the Just One, and shouldest hear the voice of his mouth. For thou shalt be his witness unto all men of what thou hast seen and heard. And now why tarriest thou? Arise, and be baptized, and wash away thy sins, calling on the name of the Lord.'"

When I had finished reading I looked at Bruno, who was weeping. "What is it?" I asked.

"The Acts of the Apostles," Bruno answered. "But altered. This is the story of the conversion of Saul of Tarsus — St. Paul the Apostle — but they've doctored it so it would seem that it was Bushistotle, not St. Paul, who was converted."

"You mean born again?"

"In a sense."

"Bushistotle was born again?"

"That's what this story reads."

"But how, when Jesus hadn't even been born yet? How could he become a born-again Christian when there wasn't even a Christ?"

"That is the nefariousness of the plot," Bruno said. "Bernie thinks he's working on a plan to have Bushistotle beatified, which would be bad enough but we might be able to live with that. But Bernie only knows half of what's going on. Or a third or less. My information is that the real plan is to have Bushistotle declared a prophet."

"A prophet?"

"Maybe even <u>the</u> Prophet. I'm not 100% sure yet, but I think so."

"<u>The</u> prophet?"

"The Messiah."

"The Savior?"

"Yup."

I took a deep breath, sat down on the concrete bench; Bruno sat beside me and began to weep heavily. Now as a general rule I don't take all these Bible stories very seriously, but when they're inculcated into your psyche from childhood, and when you're promised eternal damnation if you don't conform (or at least say you believe if anybody asks, or you want to run for office), then residual doubts about being an agnostic always remain, and this case was no exception. Although it is true that most of the world is not Christian, and that some non-Christian religions don't even have a god, and that many religions have many gods, and so it seems unlikely that any moderately compassionate god of any persuasion would punish nonbelievers just for being nonbelievers if only because a) it would be exhausting since there are so many of them, and b) it would ultimately be pointless because they wouldn't understand what they were being punished for, nonetheless doubts about damnation remain. But despite those doubts I found it insulting if what Bruno said was true, that through this evil plot the Church was going to take Jesus away from me as my Savior even though I didn't believe it, and anoint Bushistotle in his place: I have an irrational fondness for Jesus that I have never been able to make go away.

"So you mean that the new Church dogma is going to be that Bushistotle was put here on earth to save mankind?" I asked.

Bruno tried to compose himself. "Best I can make out, yes," he sniffled. "As I said I don't have full information yet because I don't know everybody else in The Matrix...."

"The matrix?"

"That's what we call ourselves: 'The Matrix.' It's a big Church thing related to the virgin birth. You know, 'womb,' 'Holy Grail,' 'sangrail,' Mary Magdalene, Keanu Reeves, whatever. Our aim is to smuggle out the truth that we know about Bushistotle, before the Vatican's giant P.R. machine can make him out to be something that he wasn't, like the savior of the world. Read this text closely and you'll see what I mean: 'I am verily a man taught according to the perfect manner of the law of the fathers, and was zealous toward our gods, as ye all are this day.'"

"It doesn't sound at all like the Bushistotle I'm translating according to the original text," I said. "His favorite word is 'binarialism.'"

"That's one point," Bruno said, "but making him sound a lot smarter than he actually was is relatively easy: a 10-year old would sound smarter. But this text is talking about Bushistotle's belief in the old Greek gods, but it then goes on and says, 'And I persecuted this way unto the death, binding and delivering into prisons both men and women,' which is talking about the atrocities committed against Persian prisoners during his invasion for their not believing in his gods. Then he says that he 'went to Persia, to bring them which were there bound unto Patmos, for to be punished,' which is talking about his illegal detention of prisoners on the island of Patmos, which was a penal colony."

"He admits that?"

"Yes, but then he says: 'And it came to pass, that, as I made my journey, and was come nigh unto Byzantium about noon, suddenly there shone from heaven a great light round about me,' which is basically when God appeared before him and he became a Christian: 'And I said, "What shall I do, Lord?" And the Lord said unto me,

"Arise, and go unto Byzantium; and there it shall be told thee of all things which are appointed for thee to do.""

"So it was God who told Bushistotle to invade Byzantium?"

"You read the words yourself, no?"

And there it was, before my eyes: Bushistotle is told by God to enter Byzantium, to save it. "What about his crucifixion?" I asked. "I'd love to get my hands on the part about Bushistotle's crucifixition."

"I haven't seen it yet," Bruno said, "but I'm sure it's coming. What they're doing is they're taking the original ancient texts whatever their source and they're altering them, rewriting them specifically for Bushistotle. This one is the conversion of Saul of Tarsus, for instance."

"All this just so U-2 can be beatified?" I asked.

"Like I said, this is much bigger than that, because then they're translating the documents back into the original biblical languages—Greek, Aramaic, whatever—and they're creating forgeries…"

"Like the Shroud of Turin?"

"…exactly, for publicity purposes, which they're going to claim were found in the Vatican Secret Archives. And it's based on these forgeries that they're going to announce that Jesus Christ wasn't actually the Savior of the world, but Bushistotle was, and Bushistotle's actions were justified because it's what God told him to do. Just read it—according to this new text, Bushistotle was the Chosen One: 'The God of our fathers hath chosen thee, that thou shouldest know his will, and see him the Just One, and shouldest hear the voice of his mouth.'"

"God speaks directly to Bushistotle?"

"Seems so, because God then goes on and tells him: 'Arise, and go unto Byzantium,' which he did."

"Where he can spread 'Truth, Goodness, and the Athenian Way?'"

"Exactly."

"And establish 'One Nation under the Gods?'"

"Yes," Bruno said, "but with this new text about Bushistotle's conversion.…"

"Being reborn?"

"…exactly, it then becomes 'One Nation under God.' Bushistotle then becomes the first crusader."

"Before U-2?"

"Right. But think of the logical conclusion: if Bushistotle is proclaimed the Savior, then what's got to happen to fulfill the prophesies?"

"Uhm.... Uhm.... Uhm.... How's about, uhm, he's got to come back to earth and save it from the Antichrist?"

"Exactly!" Bruno exclaimed. "According to this new doctrine, because he's the Savior Bushistotle has got to come back to earth and save it from the Antichrist. He'll have to retake Byzantium after a fierce battle with the devil: Saladin. So once Bushistotle returns to earth he'll have to find himself a modern-day Saladin, and that will be the prophysied Battle of Armageddon. It will destroy the world."

"Which means that Bushistotle will return..."

"...to reconquer Byzantium."

"But Byzantium is in a Muslim country today! Would any Christian actually be so stupid as to attack a Muslim country for no reason? They'd think it was a new crusade!"

"Somebody who thinks he's God would."

"So according to the new Church doctrine, Bushistotle's return marks the end of the world?"

"Correct," Bruno said, "which would make the biblical prophesies self-fulfilling. We believe that Bushistotle's return is imminent. What I mean is that the Church is going to declare that a new Bushistotle walks among us, created in the image of the ancient Philosopher-Warrior-King, but taking the place of Jesus."

"Sidelining Jesus?"

"Sidelining Jesus, and we can't allow that to happen. That's where you come in."

"Me? By what, playing God, too?"

"By changing history, no," Bruno said. "That's what Task Force B.S. is doing. What I want is for you to help us get the real truth about Bushistotle out before this evil plan to distort the historical truth gets any further. Are you willing?"

I hesitated.

"Bushistotle was <u>not</u> the Savior," Bruno said.

"No," I answered. "I don't think he was."

"And we can't allow people to be led to believe that he was."

"No."

"That would be immoral."

"Yes," I said.

"And we certainly can't prophesy that he's going to come back to save the world again, because that would be a truly horrible experience for all of us."

"Imagine living through Bushistotle again!"

"But it could be worse," Bruno said. "For all we know somebody might beat the Church to the punch, some nutcase living today might claim that he's Bushistotle resurrected, and has come to save the world by declaring war and invading foreign countries, ostensibly for their own good and for the sake of world peace, all in the name of his own personal god."

"That would be worse."

"And very harmful," Bruno said. "Are you willing to help us?"

I hesitated again.

"Are you?"

"If I help you out, will you help me get out of here alive?"

"I can," Bruno responded.

After a moment I said, "What do I have to do?"

"The instructions are in your crucifix," Bruno answered, and before I could even ask, "What crucifix?" he hugged me. Then, in what must have been a fit of passion or a coldly calculated nice try, Bruno tried to kiss me on the lips.

"I'm sorry," I said to him, pushing him back. "I'm happy to help you with your project to prevent lies from being spread about Bushistotle in exchange for getting me out of here, but I really don't do the tonsured look."

Bruno was crestfallen over my rejection of him, and although I rarely think that honesty is the best policy, it always is when my lips are involved: I'd rather kiss a St. Bernard than kiss a Dominican friar, and I'm sure that most people would agree with me.

As we left the tunnel we had a dance of "After you," "No, after you." "Please, after you," "No, I insist, after you": I was just as determined that Bruno should lead the way out as Bruno was determined that I should, but there was no way in hell that I was going to have my backside, exposed as it would have been because we had to bend over to get out on account of the low clearance, within grasp of Brother Bruno's brotherly grasp. I won in the end (pun intended) and Bruno led the way; his wagging ass in my face was again not a pretty sight, but it was better than having my pretty ass groped.

By the time we returned to the Secret Archives, Bruno had grown cold toward me, and spoke brusquely: "Your instructions are in your crucifix," he snapped. "The one newly hung on your cell wall."

"Hey, Brune," I tried to plead. "Don't be sore. It's not your fault! It's just a personal thing: I don't do tonsured."

"Hmm," Bruno huffed.

"I'll still help you if you help me," I said.

"Hmm."

Bruno brought me back to the Isolation Booth without speaking a word; there, Sister Mary Subjugation—I mean Sister Penelope—was waiting for me; Bruno provided an excuse—that Cardinal Bernie had asked to see me—and I continued to translate as best I could which, as I have often admitted, was not very good at all. Later that night, after a hearty meal in the Vatican Refectory of spinach lasagna and spicy meatballs, washed down with half a bottle of Chianti and topped off with Neapolitan ice cream—the chocolate-vanilla-and-strawberry-all-in-one-box kind that I absolutely adore—I returned to the Vice-Presidential Cell to find my "instructions." I looked at the gigantic wall-mounted crucifix from afar, then approached it, took it off the wall. No, there were no instructions on the back, on the top, or on the sides. I twisted Jesus' head but it didn't unscrew, though the thorns were kind of pointy; I tried to wiggle the INRI thing that nobody knows what it means first to the left then to the right, but it wouldn't budge an inch. Finally I tapped on the nails in his feet and hands—to what end I don't know—but they neither opened nor did blood squirt out. I was thankful for that because I didn't have access to eBay so I wouldn't be able to auction off a bleeding crucifix (which could have made me a fortune!), and would only have been stuck cleaning up the blood.

Imagine if the blood had squirted into my eye! Yuck!

Then, in what I can only categorize as a Divine Intervention, as I was replacing the cross on the wall the back slid open and revealed two candles, a vial of perfume, small slips of onionskin note paper each about the size of a cigarette paper, and a pen. *How handy*, I thought, but then I remembered from my early days of inculcation that Catholic Gift Shoppes sold crucifixes with hidden compartments where you could stash away candles and holy water, I guess in case you had to give blessings-on-the-go, or save the parish priest from making emergency extreme unction house calls on his day off, or, from a more Survivalist perspective, prep yourself for the Judgment Day: how could Jesus turn you down if you had just bathed yourself in holy water and lit a pair of dripless tapers, regardless of your sordid past? I saw no way out of it for him—a real Catch-22—so I opened the vial and held it up to my nose. There was no odor so I was sure I was handling holy water, and the apparently-holy candles were unscented, too, which was okay by me because the scented kind always gives me headaches.

After a brief interlude of rapid-fire cogitation regarding what to do with all this Catholic paraphernalia I decided to go the Survivalist route since no one would know, and keep the candles and water on hand just in case, remaining ever-on-the-lookout for matches, which weren't included in the kit. It did cross my mind that I might be too nervous to light candles if I did come face-to-face with God, but I immediately dismissed the thought as unnecessarily defeatist.

Pleased with my Pre-Day-of-Reckoning Survivalist Plan, I then found my "Matrix" instructions written in miniature calligraphy on a sheet that had been wedged behind the candles: "Dear Steve: Invent texts favorable to Bushistotle. Record the real translations on these sheets, and hide them here. Wait for further instructions. Love, Bruno." The "Love, Bruno" business was obviously pre-rejection and I admired his confidence, but deep down I hoped he'd learn not to take it personally because I really envied his handwriting, and might even ask for lessons. Then I remembered that my "You are in mortal danger" and "You are being held prisoner" notes had been written in calligraphy, as well! Pure coincidence? Perhaps. But maybe Bruno had been trying to help me all along, and I was unable to see it!

The next morning Sister Penelope picked me up at the Vice-Presidential Cell, and I found her unusually animated for a nun who'd taken a vow of silence. "Whassup?" I asked her, but of course got no answer back. Yet there was a discernible twinkle in her eye: maybe she'd gotten a promotion to "Mother" Penelope or been asked to play Sally Field, but there would be no way for me ever to find out.

Sister Naomi had already left my jelly donuts and coffee in the Isolation Booth for me. Between that and pasta every night I was as big as a house, or so I felt, but I gobbled them up nonetheless. Sister Penelope then opened up the ancient text to the next chapter, whence I would begin my translation. I scanned the text, however, and it was damning: apparently—at least according to the text—Bushistotle and the Athenian forces were in retreat, in spite of Saladin's capture:

Notwithstanding the technological superiority of the Athenian Armed Forces, Bushistotle's war is not going well: Saladin's capture has turned him into a martyr, and an insurgency has been born that threatens the stability of Byzantium, this because, unforeseen by the Athenian philosophers at the time they declared war, the Persians were not quite as keen to accept "Truth, Goodness and the Athenian Way" as they had figured. Volunteers are pouring into Byzantium from all the many provinces of Persia, and they threaten to overwhelm the Coalition forces. Casualties have been high.

I read the text aloud to Sister Penelope. "We can't publish this, Sister," I said, following my Task Force B.S. instructions. "It doesn't portray Bushistotle in a good light."

Sister Penelope looked at me, then reached into her pocket and took out a felt-tipped pen. "Cardinal Lei insists that the message be positive," she wrote on her palm. She then spit on it and rubbed the letters off on her habit.

This communication was very out of character, and a violation of her vows. It caught me off guard, as well: I'd never seen a nun write on her hand before, or spit before, except when playing softball. "Why are you writing on your hand?" I asked her. "And spitting? When did nuns learn to spit?"

"The computer is now being monitored interactively," she wrote.

"I need to communicate but can't." Then she spit on her hand again and erased what she had written.

"Did I get you in trouble for sending an email?" I asked.

"They know," she wrote. "It is a violation of my vows." Then she spit, and rubbed.

I wanted to confide in her, I wanted to tell her what my Matrix instructions were, but Bruno's words in the men's room rang between my ears: *Trust no one*. Yes it was true that she had let me use Google to look up Ακαδημια, and to send out one lonely email to my mother asking about my cats, but that was not evidence enough of her loyalty to the truth as I saw it for me to place any confidence in her: she was, after all, part of the Bushistotle plot! I decided to move ahead with my task. "We need to rewrite this," I told Sister Penelope. "I need a story of a triumphant entry into Byzantium."

Sister Penelope pulled a Bible out of her habit, flipped through a few pages and opened to where Jesus enters Jerusalem and is joyously received by the multitude. Of course nothing could be further from the truth about Bushistotle's invasion of Byzantium—the historical texts all say that the Persians and the other nations of the world bar Athens loathed him, and even in Athens he wasn't much liked—but if rewritten this way it would put a positive spin onto what Bushistotle did, and make it seem like his actions were ordained by God. That, in any case, would be the official Task Force B.S. storyline, and I was obligated to follow it.

A tear slid slowly down Sister Penelope's face, and I was uncharacteristically touched. "You don't really want me to use this story, do you?" I asked her.

"It is not mine to want," she wrote, then spit, and rubbed. "I have taken a vow of obedience." Then she spit and rubbed again.

I haven't, I thought, but I was being held incommunicado and had been warned that I was in mortal danger, so my best chance of survival, I reckoned, was to do as I was told, bide my time and hope I would avoid sainthood. Perhaps Bruno would help me escape, too, without me having to get intimate with him. That was something I would have to work on.

First, however, the text: I read the entire Jesus-into-Jerusalem story and worked out a Bushistotle-into-Byzantium angle. It would take more than just changing the names, however, so I would have to be creative: I needed to set the scene, and turn Jesus' noble voice into Bushistotle's dopey one, else no one would believe it was the same person speaking. I decided to begin right after Bushistotle's having "seen the light" in the Saul of Tarsus story, which was a great segue and bound to convince people of the ultimate goodness of Bushistotle's foreign campaigns, at least in the words of Task Force B.S.:

In the early morning hours Bushistotle prepared for His triumphant march through Byzantium, to take His rightful place as Emperor of Persia. He sent Rumsfeldiavelli and Constantina from His encampment at the Hagia Sophia in search of an ass on whose back He would ride in His Investiture Procession thence to the Imperial Palace. "Head three blocks south, turn left, walk one block, knock three times on the third door in, and there you will find an ass tied to a post," Bushistotle told them. "The ass's name is Dudley, and no one has ever sat upon him, and on his back I shall ride to the Imperial Palace."

Sister Penelope interrupted me. "There was no Hagia Sophia back then," she wrote on her hand, then spit, then rubbed.

"Who's going to know?" I asked. "The international press? Do you think that they're really going to do any independent investigation into this? No! They're just going to report what their government sources tell them, which of course is the official line!"

Sister Penelope nodded in agreement; I continued:

"But," Constantina *protested, "what if we are accused of stealing someone's ass?"*

"You shall tell your accusers that Bushistotle has need of their ass, and He is taking what is rightfully His, which is anything that He wants: it is His mandate!"

"I like bringing Dudley into the scene," I told Sister Penelope. "Dudley the Donkey meant a lot to Bushistotle, and I don't think he could be without him."

Then I continued: *Constantina and Rumsfeldiavelli obeyed, and forthwith they brought back Dudley the ass. Bushistotle looked at the ass, disappointed. "Are you sure you knocked on the right door?" He asked Constantina and Rumsfeldiavelli.*

"I think we made a wrong turn," Rumsfeldiavelli *said, "but all the goddamned signs are written in Persian, so who can tell?"*

"No matter!" Bushistotle proclaimed. "Soon they shall be writ in English!" Bushistotle paused. "Wait! 'Writ.' Is that right? 'Writ?'"

"It is, Honorable Bushistotle," Rumsfeldiavelli *assured him.*

"Should we say Greek instead of English?" Sister Penelope wrote, then she spit, and rubbed.

"We'd lose our audience," I answered. "Who's going to want to read this thing in Greek?"

Sister Penelope didn't seem entirely convinced, but I pressed ahead anyway.

"I'm sorry about the ass, Honorable Bushistotle," Constantina said. "We're doing what we can with limited on-the-ground information."

I turned to Sister Penelope. "Intelligence is everything," I said, and this time I'm sure I spied a Mona Lisa smile on her.

I began to translate again, but suddenly I recalled that I was forgetting half my charge: I was supposed to be memorizing the actual text so I could write it on the small slips of onionskin and store it in my crucifix for posterity's (and Bruno's) sake, but thus far I had only invented a new story.

Now honestly, I was never good at memorizing things, and I can barely remember other people's names, never mind my own, but here my task was doubly difficult: I had to read the biblical account of Jesus entering Jerusalem and make it Bushistotle-into-Byzantium friendly, while at the same time reading the original ancient Greek text trying to decipher what it meant when I didn't even recognize most of the letters, never mind the words, then memorize my mangled English translation of it.

Never one to let boring details get in the way, I began: *Notwithstanding the technological superiority of the Athenian Armed Forces, Bushistotle's war is not going well....*

Then, while repeating this mantra silently to myself, I had to continue inventing my fake pro-Bushistotle story: *"No matter!" Bushistotle proclaimed again. "Whether this ass is actually Dudley as was prophesied or not, it's good enough to mostly fulfill the words of Karen the Oracle: 'Tell ye the daughter of Zion: Behold, thy Savior cometh unto thee in Byzantium, riding upon an ass named Dudley!' We'll just rebaptize him Dudley, that's all, and there you have it: one more prophesy fulfilled!"*

Could I say this, I wondered? Adding Karen the Oracle at Delphi to my text? It was documented in Jesus' genealogy, I thought, so what the hay!

Then I memorized: *Notwithstanding the technological superiority of the Athenian Armed Forces, Bushistotle's war is not going well...,* when Sister Penelope tapped me on the shoulder.

"The Bible says 'ass,' but it could be 'colt,' too," she wrote on her hand, then spit, then rubbed. "Same word," spit and rub.

"Yes, but 'ass' sounds a lot funnier," I said.

"But there is significance in the choice!" Sister Penelope wrote. Then she spit and rubbed, though I noticed that some of the "!" remained.

"Significance?"

"Ass = peace," Sister Penelope wrote, then spit and rubbed, "colt = war, symbolism," she continued, then spit and rubbed.

"Dudley is the ass of peace?" I asked.

Sister Penelope nodded yes.

So according to my story Bushistotle is entering Byzantium in peace? Far from the truth, of course, but humor is humor: "Yes," I said, "but who knows that ass equals peace anymore? To me an ass is an ass, just like it is to most people, and it's a lot funner than a colt, and far closer to the truth, so ass it will remain."

I continued with my translation: *Then Bushistotle set about to inspect his ass in detail.*

"But Honorable Guys, really," Bushistotle complained, "I'm gonna need a mighty thick saddle because this Dudley here is on his last leg, and his back is sagging like an upside-down camel."

I looked at Sister Penelope; she seemed to have no further comments because she was busy trying to rub the rest of the "!" off. *Notwithstanding the technological superiority of the Athenian Armed Forces, Bushistotle's war is not going well*, I memorized. I then felt confident enough to move on to the next phrase. *...Saladin's capture has turned him into a martyr, and an insurgency has been born that threatens the stability of Byzantium....*

Trying to keep this phrase in mind, I continued inventing the entirely fake true Legend of Bushistotle: *With that the Honorable Powellonius took off his coat and set it upon Dudley's back. The Honorable Ashcroftus did the same, as did the Honorable Cheneyon and the Honorable Constantina. Then the Honorable Coterie lifted the Honorable Bushistotle into the air and sat him thereupon, and He rode Dudley out of the Hagia Sophia into the street, with his Coterie and lots of security guards at his side.*

Then I repeated to myself: *Saladin's capture has turned him into a martyr, and an insurgency has been born that threatens the stability of Byzantium....*

I wrote: *A great and thankful multitude had come to watch the Investiture of Bushistotle as Emperor of Persia. With the help of a timber multinational to which Bushistotle's Interior Department had recently granted harvesting rights throughout Anatolia and the Levant, including the near-extinct cedars of Lebanon, the multitude took copious amounts of palm fronds that had been destined for pulping; they set them down upon the road as Bushistotle proceeded toward the Imperial Palace.*

I repeated to myself: *Notwithstanding the technological superiority of the Athenian Armed Forces, Bushistotle's war is not going well. Saladin's capture has turned him into a martyr, and an insurgency has been born that threatens the stability of Byzantium....*

I wrote: *The multitude cried out: "Hosanna! Blessed is He who comes in the name of the Greeks!"*

Sister Penelope stepped on my foot. "Ouch!"

"This is blasphemous!!!" Sister Penelope wrote on her palm. Then she spit and rubbed then spit and rubbed again; she wrote the "!!!" so hard that I think she actually hurt herself, but at the same time, perpetual penitent that she was, I don't think she was as averse to self-mortification as I am, so she mightn't have minded.

"But this was your idea!" I said, and she stepped on my foot again. "Ouch!"

"!!!" she wrote.

Then TWANG! I heard: an Instant Message.

"FUCK!" I shouted. "Christ!"

Now cursing is not in my nature (much), but I felt entirely justified in this instance because a) the TWANG! had scared me half to death, and b) it had caused me to completely forget what it was that I was trying to memorize. *Notwithstanding the technological....*

Damn!

Then I looked at the Instant Message, which read: "Achim sadoc abiud amon zorobabel." This meant that it could have only come from Sister Naomi, and best I could tell it meant "Danger Will Robinson!" I felt my arms about to flail rigidly in front of me, but got distracted because as soon as Sister Penelope saw the Instant Message she whipped a cell phone out of her habit—you gotta wonder how much they can store under those bulky raiments, don't you?—and began furiously thumbing an instant response back, in further flagrant violation of her vows, and the house "*Divieto di Usare Telefonini*" rules.

But boy could that nun's thumbs fly!

Then TWANG! Another Instant Message, this one reading "abia asa josaphat joram ozias joatham achaz," and Sister Penelope furiously thumbed another instant response back.

Wait! I thought. *Achim Sadoc Abiud Amon Zorobabel Abia Asa Josaphat Joram Ozias Joatham Achaz.* I remembered those words, and thought. Suddenly I shrieked to myself *Oh my God! The reputed ancestors of Jesus, I mean Bushistotle!* This concerned me: could it be that I had been mis-reflating Sister Naomi's mumblings back into English, and she wasn't mumbling the things that I thought she was saying as they are herein being reported? Or was this some secret cabbalistic code among members of Task Force B.S. that I had not been told of?

Sister Penelope shoved her cell phone back under her habit, furiously licked the palm of her hand and rubbed it repeatedly against her habit, erasing all evidence of her silent conversation with me. She finished just in time, too: Cardinal Bernie was making his rounds, and he tapped on the fishbowl window.

Sister Penelope let him in; he approached me and slapped me on the back: "How ya' doin', Stevie-boy?"

"Fine, Your Eminence," I answered. "Just rewriting history, that's all, doing my small part for Task Force B.S."

"Good for you," the cardinal said. "And remember, 'Bernie' is just fine...."

"Okay, Bernie."

"Let me see how you're doing." Bernie put his reading glasses on, approached the computer screen, ran his finger along the line that read *The multitude cried out: "Hosanna! Blessed is He who comes in the name of the Greeks!"*

"This 'He' Bushistotle?" he asked.

"Yes, sir," I said.

"Excellent, excellent!" Bernie cried. "You're well on your way to canonization, Stevie-boy, toeing the old Task Force B.S. lie!"

"Line?" I asked.

Bernie chuckled. "Remember," he said, "we don't want to turn him into the Messiah, just a saint!"

"Right!" I answered, but I found his comment foreboding.

Then Bernie made to leave, but not before Sister Penelope

kneeled before him and kissed his ring. "Good you remembered proper protocol, Sister," he said, and he was gone.

Briefly I returned to my translation, or should I say my invention: *The multitude cried out: "Hosanna! Blessed is He who comes in the name of the Greeks!"* and I finished off the paragraph—*Bushistotle was humbled, at least to a degree: "Aw, shucks, guys! It's nothing!" He claimed, but in His Heart of Hearts He knew the Goodness of His acts.*

Sister Penelope did not interrupt my writing, and for a time I decided not to try to memorize the semi-real text that I was sort of translating from ancient Greek while I was simultaneously trying to invent a Bushistotle Legend that would be approved by Task Force B.S.:

Bushistotle adjusted himself in His makeshift saddle, wished He could find some stirrups and spurs to get His ass on the move: He had miracles to perform in Byzantium, and processions could be tedious, even if they were good P.R.! Some of the multitude who had come to meet Him, however, overcome with joy at having been liberated from the Persians, began to place articles of their clothing in His path, lest poor old Dudley hurt his ancient hoofs on the uneven cobblestone surface. "No!" cried Bushistotle to the crowd. "No! Disrobe not! Keep your clothes on! Standards of decency are about to be instituted, now that the heathen Persians have been routed!"

The multitude obeyed, and Dudley brayed in joy, for the crowd was not a pretty lot.

And as Bushistotle and His Coterie were drawing nigh upon the Imperial Palace, Bushistotle whispered to Rumsfeldiavelli: "Honorable Rumsfeldiavelli, what is the status of the Weapons of <u>Mass</u> Destruction here in Byzantium? I saw no evidence of them in the Hagia Sophia."

"Uhm, you mean the plagues that we were absolutely certain that the Persians had?" Rumsfeldiavelli asked.

"Precisely," said Bushistotle. "Now that we have entered Byzantium, I have a speech to make."

Cheneyon interrupted the conversation. "Honorable Bushistotle," he said, "we continue our search, they could be anywhere. Buried in the sand or hidden away in the mountains, or even at the bottom of the sea, just waiting to be lifted. In the meantime we have to remember that the Saladin regime was evil, and a threat to global stability."

"Do you think we'll find any WMD's in the Imperial Palace?" Bushistotle asked.

"There are none," said Ashcroftus.

"Hmm," Bushistotle bristled. "Just like Karen prophesied."

"But we are 'interviewing' some prisoners, and are certain that we will have better intelligence shortly," added Ashcroftus.

"Then what shall I say to the multitude?" Bushistotle asked.

"Repeat after me," said Cheneyon. "We have to remember that the Saladin regime was evil, and a threat to global stability."

"We have to remember that the Saladin regime was evil, and a threat to global stability," repeated Bushistotle.

"Excellent, Honorable Bushistotle," Cheneyon said. "Excellent!"

Here I thought I had outdone myself, and felt perversely proud: I had single-handedly managed not only to rewrite history, but I had created an entirely new justification for Bushistotle's invasion of Persia!

I turned to Sister Penelope, pointed at the computer screen, asked her to read it. "What do you think of this shit?" I asked her. "Will anybody believe it?"

She put her index finger in front of her lips, telling me to be quiet.

I figured she didn't like my language, so I rephrased: "Okay, Sister, let me put it this way: Will anybody believe this crap?"

Again she put her index finger in front of her lips; I tried yet again: "Do you think anybody will believe this garbage?"

Her index finger approached her lip again, and I surmised that she did not want to communicate with me. I gave up, continued with my creative pro-Bushistotle creative writing: *As the Bushistotle Coterie conversed among themselves, the gathered multitude continued to shout "Hosanna! Hosanna! Blessed is He who comes in the name of the Greeks!"*

No, no one will believe this crap, I thought, but I kept on writing it anyhow, since the creation of the Legend of Bushistotle was now up to me: *"See, Honorable Bushistotle," said Cheneyon. "I told you we would be welcomed as liberators!"*

"Hear, hear!" said Constantina.

"Hear, hear!" said Rumsfeldiavelli.

"Hear, hear!" said Ashcroftus.

Then there was silence among the Coterie, despite the roar of the multitude.

"Honorable Powellonius?" asked Bushistotle.

"Yes, Honorable Bushistotle?"

"Are you not here?"

"Here, sir!" said Powellonius. "Here!"

And Dudley the Donkey brayed in happiness.

At this point I just wanted to jump right inside my story and pound the living shit out of Powellonius: what a fucking wimp! I would have preferred to write Powellonius as a Brutus—actually, I would have preferred to write anyone as a Brutus—so in a sense I guess I'm no better than Task Force B.S., but as far as I could tell they had never been threatened with martyrdom as I had, just ostracism from Bushistotle's inner circle, which to me would have been no big deal, so they had no real excuse.

As the procession moved onward, I continued to write, *when Bushistotle drew nigh upon Saladin's Imperial Palace, He saw it and wept over it, knowing that it was His. Then from amongst the crowd Cassandra the drunken oracle appeared. "If thou only knewest today the things which belong unto peace, but they now are hidden from thine eyes!" she shouted to Bushistotle. "For the days shall come upon thee when thine enemies shall cast up a bank about thee, and compass thee round, and keep thee in on every side, and shall dash thee to the ground, and thy children within thee. And they shall not leave in thee one stone upon another, because thou knewest not the time of thy visitation!"*

"That woman is a real mess," Bushistotle said. "Needs a 12-Step!"

The Bushistotle Coterie agreed.

Cheneyon moved quickly then to silence the wench, motioned with his arm and set a contingent of security forces upon her, and she was never heard from again. He whispered unto the head of the security detail, "Weren't you in charge of finding a Friendly Crowd?"

"Sorry sir," the head of the security detail said. "We thought she was on our side because she makes no sense."

"Understandable," said Cheneyon. "But don't let it happen again!"

Now the palm fronds laid down before Bushistotle's ass made it difficult for poor old Dudley to walk, and he faltered a few times and the Coterie stabilized him. Then Bushistotle entered into the Imperial Palace, and when He arrived the remaining guards loyal to Saladin, who had been disarmed, said, "Who the fuck is this?"

And the multitude said, "This is Bushistotle, Emperor of Persia!"

And knowing this, the blind and the lame came before Bushistotle, now seated in Saladin's throne, and He healed them. And when He saw the great destruction wrought upon the palace He ordered infrastructure works to commence forthwith. But when the chief priests and scribes of the Saladin regime saw the wonderful things He had done, they were mighty, mighty agitated.

They said unto Him, "What the hell are you doing? You're destroying our power base!"

And Bushistotle said unto them, "Yea, did ye never read that out of the mouth of babes and sucklings thou hast perfected praise?"

But like Bushistotle himself, Saladin's chief priests and scribes had no idea what Bushistotle was talking about, and as Cassandra had prophesied they went about their business fomenting dissent and wreaking havoc upon the occupying forces, which would be forced to fight back.

At this point I took a break, turned and looked at Sister Penelope, but she barely acknowledged my presence. I turned my attention to the real text which I had been attempting to memorize, and began to work on the next sentence: *Volunteers are pouring into Byzantium from all the many provinces of Persia, and threaten to overwhelm the Coalition forces....*

Then I wrote: *Now on the morrow, Bushistotle toured the devastated city. He hungered, and saw a fig tree that bore no fruit but that gave shelter to a Saladin sniper. Bushistotle waived His arm and a member of His security detail hit the tree with a blast of napalm, and the sniper, and the tree, were gone. Bushistotle then said unto the ashes: "Let there be no fruit or snipers henceforward forever in this tree," and unsurprisingly there were none.*

Then I memorized: *Volunteers are pouring into Byzantium from all the many provinces of Persia, and threaten to overwhelm the Coalition forces....*

"See," said Constantina, who witnessed the entire event, "hardly any opposition to our invasion at all!"

Volunteers are pouring into Byzantium from all the many provinces of Persia, and threaten to overwhelm the Coalition forces....

"The road to Persepolis is now cleared!" exclaimed Rumsfeldiavelli. "The Honorable Bushistotle has defeated the enemy!"

Volunteers are pouring into Byzantium from all the many provinces of Persia, and threaten to overwhelm the Coalition forces....

Nonetheless, when Saladin's chief priests and scribes heard of Bushistotle's impiety, they sought further how they might destroy Him, for they feared Him, and they recruited more snipers, and planted more fig trees. Yet undaunted, Bushistotle was daily teaching the people the virtues of Bushistotlism, and the virtues of the Bushistotle Doctrine of Preemptive Retaliation, but the chief priests and the scribes and the principal men of the people still sought to destroy Him. "I have firmly planted the flag of liberty!" Bushistotle would cry unto the multitudes that gathered round him, and Saladin's chief priests and scribes could not find what they might do, for Bushistotle's arguments were persuasive insofar as the Armed Forces hung upon Him in a Mighty Coalition, which let Him continue His teaching.

Then I memorized *Casualties have been high....*

I wrote: *And Bushistotle spoke unto the people of Byzantium, and said: "People of Byzantium, we are led by events and common sense to one conclusion: the survival of liberty in Athens increasingly depends on the survival of liberty in other lands. Therefore, the best hope for peace in our world is the expansion of Athens throughout those lands. That is why Athens invaded Persia, and why I reluctantly declared war! It had nothing to do with those nasty nonexistent Weapons of <u>Mass</u> Destruction after all: the Saladin regime was evil, and a threat to global stability!"*

Casualties have been high....

"Hosanna!" cried the multitude. "Blessed is He who comes in the name of the Greeks!"

Casualties have been high....

"Blessed is He who comes in the name of the Greeks!"

Casualties have been high....

And faced with the popularity in Athens of Bushistotle's invasion of Persia, and overwhelmed by shock and awe, the day came when Persia's chief priests and scribes and the principal men of the people surrendered, and the multitudes of Byzantium rejoiced. And thereafter ensued the Bushistotle Era, marked in history by Peace on Earth and Goodwill toward Men.

Having written this elaborate lie I immediately understood the meaning of martyrdom, and was even more certain than before that it wasn't meant for me. But I had memorized what I had set out to, so I could put it to paper that night.

Some will accuse me of mixing my stories, which can sometimes confound the reader. Yet unto them I would say, "Ain't that what Bushistotle is all about?" To which I am certain they will find no good answer, for in the tall tale that is the Legend of St. Bushistotle Spartans have been turned into Persians and Persians have been turned into Spartans; pagans have been turned into prophets and prophets have been turned into pagans. Today has become yesterday and yesterday tomorrow, true has become false and false has become true, but at least I punctuate.

The moral? Ye shall see: never fuck with an oracle!

It was a leap of faith trusting that Bruno would help me, but I fulfilled my mission anyway because he was my best chance. I spent many more long days inventing pro-Bushistotle tripe about Bushistotle's escapades in Persia that Task Force B.S. would eat up and eventually disseminate to the public, all the while sort-of translating the original ancient texts and trying to remember what they said so I could write it down later at night on the onionskin paper that was stashed inside my crucifix. Of course my memory isn't good and my ancient Greek is even worse, so what I wound up writing on those onionskin sheets was pretty much a crock of shit, too, though some elements of the plot were indeed based on what had been written; others, of course, were subject to my faulty recollection; and others, still, were where I invented to fill in the Windex gaps, or at least that's what I would blame any inconsistencies on. But I was having a lot of fun, despite my incarceration.

I didn't hear from Bruno for a long time—exactly how many days I don't remember—and Sister Penelope had returned to her vow of silence, so I was slowly going out of my mind due to lack of human contact. Like any writer, then, I thrust myself into my tale and started to live vicariously through the story that I wove, even to the point of getting nauseous imagining myself aboard the S.S. Bushistotle, raising the "Mission Accomplished" banner. Then one evening when I returned to my cell after a long day of inventing pro-Bushistotle stories to support his beatification, I opened my wall-mounted crucifix and found another calligraphic note: "Bring your papers tomorrow, stuff them in the eggs." Though I wasn't sure what was meant and I was in the middle of Bushistotle's campaign in Persia so my story wouldn't be complete, I would obey, but not before hurrying to document what more of the campaign I had managed to sort-of memorize.

The next day, shirt pocket stuffed with onionskin slips full of my lousy handwriting in blue ballpoint ink, Sister Penelope arrived as usual at my cell. This time, however, we headed not to the Isolation Booth but back to the Vatican Refectory, which was overflowing with people I thought I recognized from among Cardinal Bernie's sundry canonization task forces that had been locked in the safe by his office. Bernie himself was seated in the center of a long table at the head of the room, and Brother Bruno was seated beside him, to his right. I waved to Bruno but he turned away; Sister Penelope dumped me in a nearby chair, and made her way to be seated by Bernie, too. Soon Sister Naomi and Mrs. Irma R. Gorgonzola arrived, and all the Task Force B.S. honchos were there.

Bernie stood; the refectory quieted. "Ladies and gentlemen," he said as Sister Penelope signed along for the deaf or those who just didn't want to listen. "Welcome. Some of you will remember a similar gathering last year, but for those of you who don't, welcome to the Second Annual College of Cardinals Easter Egg Hunt Decorating Committee meeting, which is the new Easter egg hunt I instituted right after my Rehabilitation, for P.R. purposes."

There was a roar of applause among the captive audience.

"This year as last, your task will be to decorate Easter eggs for the hunt that this pope is hosting for the College of Cardinals after Mass at Castel Gandolfo on Palm Sunday. It's sure to be a fun event, great publicity, and the international press is invited."

There was another roar of applause among the captive audience.

"This pope himself will be in charge of counting how many Easter eggs each cardinal collects if he can, and the winning cardinal will be allowed to choose which country he would like to be papal nuncio to for the next year. In case of a tie there will be a sudden-death hunt for this special golden goose egg." Bernie held up a golden egg—I assume it was a goose egg but didn't feel like hanging around this little feast to find out for sure, so I took him at his word—then he put it back in his pocket. "Of course if the winning cardinal cannot fulfill his papal nuncio obligations for any reason such as death—which occurs quite frequently—the runner-up will fill his place but will be stuck with the same country, like it or not. Last year's winner, Cardinal Liguri..." There was yet another roar of applause from among the captive audience when Cardinal Liguri's wheelchair was pushed in front of the head table, which applause Bernie did his best to interrupt. "People, people," he said, clapping his hands for emphasis. "Please, please! There is much work for us to do today!" The captive applause died down. "Last year's winner, Cardinal Liguri, chose Monaco, so this year's winner will have to choose a different country. Those are the rules."

There were groans from the captive audience.

"I know, I know!" Bernie clapped again, and the groans died down. "Thank you," he continued. "Now then, you may also be aware that we are making some changes to last year's egg decorating guidelines. First, we got a lot of bad press because we used hard-boiled eggs and wound up throwing out nearly a ton of egg salad that went bad. The truth of the matter is that nobody likes hard-boiled eggs and nobody likes egg salad, just like nobody knows why hard-boiled eggs weigh so goddamned much, so this year we're going to use blown eggs."

There were groans from the captive audience, which Bernie again tried to quell. "Yes, I know, there's a trick to blowing eggs but I'm sure you'll catch on fast," he said. "But we can then freeze dry the insides and use them all year long because they won't go bad, and we'll avoid a lot of bad P.R., which is one the top priorities that this pope has tasked me with this year. Given recent events that you are probably aware of, our new campaign is called 'Exorcise Bad P.R.!'" One captive person applauded—me—but no one else joined in, so I felt like a real idiot, and slouched in my chair. "Another change," Bernie continued, "is that this year we won't be using wax because it's too reminiscent of those Orthodox people, and we don't want that symbolism. It's not the image we want to portray to the international public. Therefore, each of you is being provided with one Paas Easter egg decorating kit, which is much more Holy Roman Catholic and Apostolic in spirit."

There was modest applause from among the captive audience.

"Okay people, okay!" Bernie interrupted. "Finally, rather than trying to imitate Faberge eggs like we did last year too, which was a dismal failure I might add, this year we're going to be reproducing Old Master allegorical paintings on our eggs. Each of you will be given a tiny paintbrush for that purpose, and I expect you to do your best for our cause! The cardinals will definitely appreciate it, and think of the great press it'll generate!"

Bernie sat down again to thunderous applause. Then, an order of brothers began to hand out the Paas egg decorating kits and paintbrushes to the hundreds of us lined up at the long tables in the refectory, as well as a teacup full of warm water each that we could use to juice up the dye. Other supplies followed: a spittoon, which I assumed was to be used for the insides of the eggs we were supposed to be blowing out, and a knitting needle, which I assumed was to be used for making the holes, as well as a straw and a brown-and-yellow basket stuffed with green plastic grass where I assumed we were to deposit our creations, plus a Styrofoam carton containing the hapless victims: a dozen grade A medium-sized white eggs.

The final tool was the full-color glossy plates of the paintings we were to copy onto the eggs. Now besides the spatial problem of how to render a flat painting on an egg-shaped egg, which is, in fact, without distortion physically impossible, there was the practical problem that I can barely write my name, never mind paint a painting with Paas water-based dye, or anything else for that matter. Nor had I ever blown an egg before in my entire life, but that didn't bother me much because I figured I'd be a natural.

Well wasn't I surprised! Blowing eggs is not as easy as you might imagine nor as easy as blowing other (nameless) things, and my first effort was a near failure. To this day I am convinced that there was a little yellow baby chicken somewhere in there clogging up the hole, but no matter how hard I blew I was unable to find even a trace of a feather. Some people were lucky and did wind up with chickens, and others got double yolks, but unfortunately it wasn't my day, and all I wound up with was eggs.

The first work of art I was commissioned to reproduce on an egg was the by-now-cliché Michelangelo rendition of the Creation reproduced on posters in every gay household in America and perhaps beyond, with God lightly touching Adam's finger with his own: how queer! My first task before embarking upon my painting career, however, was to hollow out the egg, which I had no idea how to do; there being no set rules against copying, I watched what my more experienced neighbors were doing: they tapped lightly on one end of the egg with the knitting needle, then they tapped lightly on the other end of the egg with that selfsame knitting needle, until two holes were made. Some then used the straw, others just put their lips to the egg and blew the insides out, right into the handy nearby spittoon. Yum, wouldn't those make delicious omelets?!

So I tried my hand—or mouth—at the task, and using the knitting needle I prospected the ends of the egg with the care of a miner hunting diamonds, then put my lips to the egg, and blew.

Nothing.

I blew again.

Nothing.

I blew again, hard this time, my face turning blue, but still nothing. The people around me were already starting their painting, and I still had an incipient chicken stuck inside my egg.

I shook the damned egg; nothing. I cursed silently at it; nothing. I tried a prayer—*Our Father who art in Heaven, help me hollow this egg*—but nothing. So I tried the straw, inserted it gently, blew, but nothing. *This isn't working*, I thought, so I tried my hand at some reverse-psychology: I sucked, my logic being that sucking is more natural than blowing, and easier on the lungs. At first there was some resistance, but then I felt some albumin (the technical name for the white part, in case you didn't know) ooze into my mouth. Oooh, I was enjoying this. I sucked harder, then I felt the yellow stuff. Oooh, I was enjoying this even more. So then I sucked harder still, and I felt more white stuff, and I sucked harder and harder, until the egg had released everything it had inside of it.

Wow, I thought, *neat*, and of course I was exhausted and wanted a cigarette (and I don't even smoke), but now I had a mouthful of raw egg, and what was I going to do with that? Salmonella being what it is, I daren't swallow despite my natural inclination to do so, so I shot a furtive glance around the room and when the least number of people were looking, I spit the egg into the spittoon. Yet again, wouldn't it make a delicious omelet?!

My next task was to paint, so I took my Paas kit and did what I could: the two hands I wound up painting looked like those suckling pigs you're forced to dissect in high school, but no matter: in my mind the effort counted more than the result. Then I took the first slip of paper containing the true story of Bushistotle's escapades in Persia as I saw it out of my pocket, rolled it up and inserted it into the egg hole, thinking *in the beginning was their word, but their word had no meaning*....

Part 1:

Notwithstanding the technological superiority of the Athenian Armed Forces, Bushistotle's war is not going well: Saladin's capture has turned him into a martyr, and an insurgency has been born that threatens the stability of Byzantium, this because, unforeseen by the Athenian philosophers at the time they declared war, the Persians were not quite as keen to accept "Truth, Goodness and the Athenian Way" as they had figured. Volunteers are pouring into Byzantium from all the many provinces of Persia, and threaten to overwhelm the Coalition forces. Casualties have been high.

Our fearless Philosophers are meeting at the Round Table below deck on the S.S. Bushistotle, now dry-docked in the safety of the harbor at Patmos, a small island in an archipelago off the Turkish coast, just north of the island of Rhodes, to undertake urgent repairs and try to figure out what to do next. The "Mission Accomplished: Thank You Bushistotle" banner, hand-embroidered by Mrs. Bushistotle in honor of her husband, was being lowered; it had been torn in an accident, and it now read merely, "Mission Accomplished: Thank You Bushi."

"Hail, Bushistotle!" *said Rumsfeldiavelli.*

"Forget that, Honorable Rumsfeldiavelli," *said Bushistotle.* "A fine mess you've gotten us into now! You promised the plague of yellow frogs would work, but now we're facing this insurgency!"

"Who knew the frogs would be killed by the red tide algae?" *said Rumsfeldiavelli.*

"And weren't the people of Byzantium to have died of thirst?" *asked Bushistotle.*

"Our intelligence didn't pick up on the fact that they had built a system of underground reservoirs with a several-year supply of potable water for the city," *Rumsfeldiavelli said.* "It was hard to foresee: we thought they were subways."

"It was hard to foresee, or you didn't foresee it?" *asked Cheneyon.*

"I saw it!" *said Powellonius.* "I knew they wouldn't give in so easily."

"Shut up, Powellonius," *said Constantina.* "No one listens to you; you are so contrarian."

"I repeat," *said Cheneyon.* "Was it hard to foresee, or didn't you foresee it?"

"Same thing, no?" *said Rumsfeldiavelli.*

This first installment of the truish history of Bushistotle as somewhat written in the ancient texts now inserted inside my newly painted egg, I placed it on the green plastic grass in my brown-and-yellow basket, and it was on its way; I felt like Kevin Costner in Message in a Bottle, and wondered whether Brother Bruno would rescue me.

I started on my second egg, tapped on it and blew, but this time the egg was much more amenable to extrication, and it flew right out of its shell and into my spittoon. *Plop!* Two eggs down, and I started to Paas-paint again, this time Raffaello Sanzio's Faith, Hope, Charity, who were each flanked by two cherubim. Personally I like cherubim—who, in case you ever run into one on the street, do in fact outrank seraphim in the celestial order of things—so I decided to put most of my effort on them; time being short, I winged the three ladies, pardon the pun, who wound up bearing a remote resemblance to three of my cousins with the exact same names, each of whom got married in a shotgun wedding.

I inserted the next installment:

Part 2:

"Now look where we are," Bushistotle said. "Stuck here in a quagmire on this godforsaken dump of an island Pastos...."

"Patmos," said Ashcroftus.

"Pagmos," said Bushistotle. "A penile colony, of all places, with a hole in the side of our flagship, the S.S. Bushistotle. This is a dangerous situation."

"We're fucked," said Cheneyon.

"Honorable Cheneyon!" exclaimed Ashcroftus.

"I'm sorry, Honorable Ashcroftus, but it's true," Bushistotle said. "We're fucked. On top of the war, our backup plan, the plague of cockroaches, got loose in Athens. What a way to run a campaign!"

"I'm not a politician, I have always said that," said Rumsfeldiavelli.

"The roaches were supposed to be our secret weapon!" said Ashcroftus.

"We're still working on changing the expiration dates on the baby formula," said Rumsfeldiavelli.

"It'll take years before that stuff goes sour—did you ever taste it?" asked Constantina. "We don't have years."

"How much longer will we be in dry dock?" asked Cheneyon.

"About a week," said Rumsfeldiavelli. "They're logging some of the near-extinct cedars of Lebanon right now to make up the planks for the repairs."

"Don't we have anything newkuler?" asked Bushistotle.

"We kicked the Atomists out for not being True Believers," said Ashcroftus. "They deny that truth is ultimately knowable."

"Just when you need them, damn!" said Bushistotle.

"Honorable Bushistotle!" cried Ashcroftus. "Your language!"

"Oh shut up!" Bushistotle shouted. "God damns things all the time, so why can't I? We're in a pickle here, and I'm waiting for that miracle that you promised."

This part of my story safely tucked away in an Easter egg, I have another confession to make: it wasn't until I was fifteen that I actually figured out why eggs have one pointy side and one not-so-pointy side. Then one day I was walking to sex education class which for some strange reason was erudition entrusted to the gym teacher, who seems like just the kind of guy you'd want to have teach your kids all the intricacies of the human reproduction system in between beers during the Pro-Bowl or something, when Bang! it hit me: eggs pop out the pointy-side first! Now didn't that just make me the star pupil of my sex education class?

My next masterpiece to copy was Cortona's <u>Vision of St. Francis</u>, and since back home I'd been known to have more than a few visions after one or two snorts too many of something I can't put in print, I figured it'd be a cinch: like all modern art, just smoke some weed, paint whatever you can, give it a fancy name like <u>Study in Nihilism #36</u> (Medium: Crap on Trashbags), and sooner or later it'll be hung in a gallery somewhere, guaranteed!

Part 3:

"I've been praying incessantly for that miracle," said Ashcroftus.

"You'd better have one mighty big prayer hole for that, 'cause we're screwed," said Cheneyon.

"How come we were so confident of victory before?" asked Bushistotle.

"Outwardly," responded Cheneyon. "But to ourselves we always knew this was a dumb idea."

"Karen forewarned me of this," Bushistotle said, "but I didn't want to believe her."

"With all due respect, Number One, I mean Chief," Cheneyon said, "my advice is never to fuck with an oracle again. She's brought you nothing but bad luck."

"Agreed," said Bushistotle. "She's been nothing but a thorn in my side, what with the paternity suit and everything, as if I'm responsible for screwing her and I have to clean up the mess. I've screwed a lot more things in my life than her, but nobody ever tried to hold me responsible for it before."

"We know, sir," said Aschroftus. "We do our best to keep you ignorant of things."

"He means out of the loop, sir," said Cheneyon.

"Thank you, Number One," said Bushistotle. "But what went wrong with the rest of our WLD's?"

"A string of bad luck," said Rumsfeldiavelli.

"We already know that," said Cheneyon.

"The pacifics, man. The pacifics," said Bushistotle.

"It was the goddamned food chain," Rumsfeldiavelli answered. "First of all I want to say CYA-wise that the red tide worked all right except for their stupid underground reservoirs, but when we launched the yellow frogs a week later we didn't know that most of them would die in the stupid red tide. The ones that didn't die wound up eating all the gnats, which really took the wind out of that sail—you'd be surprised how many gnats one frog can eat in a day."

"I can only imagine," said Powellonius.

"Of course the whole place was still littered with the bodies of dead yellow frogs and our intelligence assets report that it indeed was starting to smell pretty bad, but instead of bothering the people all the flies congregated around the frog corpses, and then they were swooped down on by an unscripted flock of birds straight out of Alfred Hitchcock. We nixed the cattle plague because our agricultural extensionists decided that if the wind started blowing the wrong way it might decimate our own herds, and that would lose farm votes. Plus it was talc anyway. In the end what happened was that there was no wind at all, so we couldn't launch our seven test tubes of boil powder—they're still in the laboratory, just in case—and when the wind did start to blow it was accompanied by buckets of rain that extinguished our firebombs and the fires we had set in the suburbs to blacken the city. The locusts wouldn't come out in the rain and most of the fields were smoldering, anyhow, so there wasn't much left for them to eat, so the SOB's just wound up sitting there and sitting there, staring at each other till they all dropped dead either of starvation or boredom—the jury's still out on that—and I've already debriefed you on the status of our devious baby formula plot."

"If anything could go wrong I guess it did," said Ashcroftus.

"You bet it did," said Rumsfeldiavelli.

Just as I completed this egg someone at the far end of the refectory shouted, "Bingo! A chicken!"

Bernie stood up. "Someone's called 'bingo' over there!"

A Vatican Swiss Guard contingent pranced gaily towards the man.

"That's not fair!" another man shouted. "I had double yolks!"

"You should have called it earlier!" Bernie said.

The head of the Vatican Swiss Guard said, "Yup, looks like a chicken to me!"

"So we have a winner!" Bernie said. "Miters off to our winner!"

And with that the audience began to clap.

I hadn't gotten a chicken, or a double yolk, nor, in fact, even a yolk with a bloodspot, so I guess I was on a real losing streak. But time was running out and everyone had way more eggs done than I had, so I decided to stick two slips of onionskin into my next egg, which was The Crowning of Charlemagne, but to be honest in the rendition given to me to copy Charlemagne bore an uncanny resemblance to Bushistotle:

Part 4:

"But we still need a way out of this," said Cheneyon.

"You sure we don't have anything newkuler," asked Bushistotle, "to defeat the insurgency?"

"Absolutely," said Rumsfeldiavelli.

"Not even a defensive weapon that we can conveniently make offensive?" asked Bushistotle. "Bomb the shit out of them?"

"Nope," said Rumsfeldiavelli. "We're stretched to the limit."

"We need to sort out where we are and we're were going from here," said Cheneyon.

"Pagmos," said Bushistotle.

"Patmos," corrected Ashcroftus.

"What is it?" asked Bushistotle.

"Patmos," Ashcroftus repeated.

"Honorable Rumsfeldiavelli," said Cheneyon, "what say our intelligence assets about the enemy at Byzantium?"

"It is a most dire, and unforeseen, situation," said Rumsfeldiavelli.

"Unforeseen again?" asked Cheneyon.

"Apparently they have been able to mount a force of 144,000 foreign and local insurgents riding red, white, black and pale green horses," said Rumsfeldiavelli. "We assume, naturally, that they dyed the red and green ones, to scare us, since we don't think there's such a thing as red or green horses."

"Naturally," said Cheneyon.

"Did it work?" asked Bushistotle. "Did they scare us?"

There was no immediate response.

"What about the fortifications?" Cheneyon asked, ignoring Bushistotle.

"According to our very limited intelligence," answered Constantina, "the insurgents are holed up in a temple surrounded by a really high wall with twelve gates. Three of the gates face east, three north, three west and three south, and the temple's wall has twelve courses of stone as its foundation, and it measures forty-four cubits high. Its foundations are decorated with every precious stone: the first course of stones is of jaspar, the second sapphire, the third chalcedony, the fourth emerald, the fifth sardonyx, the sixth carnelian, the seventh chrysolite, the eighth beryl, the ninth topaz, the tenth chrysoprase, the eleventh hyacinth, and the twelfth amethyst. The twelve gates are decorated with pearls. Our goal is to enter through the south gates, because they are the least heavily fortified."

"Why don't we just take the gems and run?" asked Bushistotle.

"I thought of that, too, Honorable Bushistotle," said Rumsfeldiavelli, "but we can't even get close to the wall. We have a force of merely 7,000."

"Why don't we have more troops on the ground?" asked Bushistotle.

"Got rid of the draft," said Rumsfeldiavelli.

"Let me clarify, Honorable Bushistotle," said Cheneyon. "The draft is unpopular, which is why we got rid of it, under Emperor Nixonious. Plus we didn't foresee having to lay siege to the temple—we were relying on the WLD's to do the job for us, based on our on-the-ground-intelligence. Otherwise, we might have reinstated it."

"Again with the 'didn't foresee,'" complained Bushistotle. "You Honorable Guys are letting me down."

Then the next installment:

<u>Part 5</u>:

Cheneyon stared angrily at Rumsfeldiavelli. "I am not the military strategist."

Ashcroftus stared angrily at Rumsfeldiavelli. "Nor am I."

Constantina stared angrily at Rumsfeldiavelli. "Nor am I."

Powellonius stared angrily at Rumsfeldiavelli. "Nor am I."

"Well don't look at me," said Bushistotle.

"I do the best I can with what I'm given," said Rumsfeldiavelli.

A page entered with a scroll and handed it to Rumsfeldiavelli. "You're not following standard protocol," Rumsfeldiavelli said to the page. "Intelligence scrolls are supposed to be protected by a contingent of MP's."

The page shrugged his shoulders; Rumsfeldiavelli opened the scroll. "That was easy," Rumsfeldiavelli said. "I usually need help opening these things."

"What does it say?" asked Bushistotle.

"No idea," Rumsfeldiavelli said. "You try, Honorable Ashcroftus." Rumsfeldiavelli handed the scroll to Ashcroftus.

"What does it say?" asked Bushistotle.

Ashcroftus read: "Achaia atque Asia falso exterrit velut Bushistotlus adventaret, vario super ejus exitu rumore eoque pluribus vivere eum fingentibus credentibusque."

"What in God's name does that mean?" asked Bushistotle.

"No clue," said Ashcroftus. "I know it's Latin, but my people broke from Rome eons ago."

"Honorable Cheneyon?" asked Bushistotle.

"Languages were never really my thing," answered Cheneyon.

"Sorry, wrong scroll," said the page, who took the scroll and exited.

After this installment, my next undertaking was to paint Judith Slaying Holofernes, which is one of my favorite paintings because of all the blood and gore: it seems that Judith cut poor old Holofernes' head off merely because he was a pagan, but though the caption on the back explained that the story was supposed to represent the victory of God over paganism, as I looked around the room at the hundreds of people coloring Easter eggs and laying them gently in bushels of green plastic grass, I doubted there had ever been such a victory.

Judith, nonetheless, would be the vessel to bear my next two installments:

Part 6:

Thereafter, a contingent of sailors immediately entered with a new scroll and handed it to Rumsfeldiavelli. "That's better," Rumsfeldiavelli said. "Proper protocol. Seven SEAL's, and I'm sure I'm going to need their help opening this up. Guys!"

The Navy SEAL's helped Rumsfeldiavelli open the scroll.

"A battle report," said Rumsfeldiavelli. "Oh, gosh, not good! The Persian insurgents now apparently control the entrance to the Dardanelles. At first they couldn't get reinforcements through because of the chain we laid across the mouth of the Golden Horn, but they greased up the bottom of their ships and they got through our blockade under the cover of dark. They are now entirely refortified and resupplied."

"Not good news," said Cheneyon.

"I am just so tired of these Persian insurgents," said Bushistotle.

"A real thorn in our side, no?" said Cheneyon.

"You break it, you own it," said Powellonius.

"Oh shut up, Honorable Powellonius," said Constantina. "You are so contrarian!"

"The insurgents are demanding our full and unconditional surrender," said Cheneyon, "or they will take their battle to Athens."

"There's no way we can speed up those cedars so we can get the S.S. Bushistotle back into shape faster?" asked Bushistotle. "I'm itching to get back there to lead our troops up Byzantium Hill!"

"You never stepped foot in Byzantium," said Rumsfeldiavelli. "We came across two tiny rowboats with one fisherman in each, and you ordered us to retreat full speed backwards. We wound up hitting a tree, tearing our sail, and running hard aground, and we had to row our way out!"

"But they could have been Spartan rowboats!" said Bushistotle. "Terrorists!"

"There are no Spartans in Persia," Powellonius said.

"But the P.R. people can put great spin on it, no, make me seem like a leader?"

"Carolus Rovus is writing stuff up now," said Cheneyon.

"With pictures of me at the helm of the S.S. Bushistotle?"

"Yup," said Cheneyon.

"With Mrs. Bushistotle's 'Mission Accomplished' banner," added Ashcroftus, "as soon as we get it resewn."

"It's at times like this that I need Mrs. Bushistotle's wise counsel," Bushistotle said. "Constantina, get out your copy of <u>Dudley</u>."

"No can do, sir," Constantina said. "It fell overboard as I was rushing to safety below deck."

"Now I'm without Mrs. Bushistotle's wise counsel!" Bushistotle said. "We need a strategy, a way out of this, and <u>Dudley</u> would have the answers!"

Then I inserted into the egg the next installment to be borne by Judith as my Holy Grail.

Part 7:

"We can just wait here in the safety of Patmos harbor," said Cheneyon.

"Hear, hear!" shouted Constantina. "Excellent plan!"

"Keep the leadership out of harm's way!" shouted Bushistotle. "Excellent!"

"With all due respect, Honorable Bushistotle," said Cheneyon, "we do need to make some key decisions on the future of this military campaign. Specifically how are we going to get ourselves the hell out of this mess."

"You're right," said Bushistotle. "So, Honorable Rumsfeldiavelli, what are we doing?"

"I've ordered some two hundred vessels protecting our colonies in Italy to reinforce the few ships that have survived at Byzantium," said Rumsfeldiavelli. "With good winds, they should be there in a week."

"Can our troops survive that long near Byzantium without reinforcements?" asked Cheneyon.

"I'm not sure," answered Rumsfeldiavelli.

"How many troops do we have?" asked Cheneyon.

"Some 20,000," said Rumsfeldiavelli, "but the Persians will have ten times that many."

"What about that cattle plague?" asked Bushistotle. "Can we use it now? We still have the test tubes, right?"

"Yes," said Cheneyon, "but I'm afraid we won't be able to get close enough to their cows to have much of an effect."

"What about the boil powder?" asked Bushistotle.

"Our forces are in close proximity," said Rumsfeldiavelli. "They'd be affected, too."

"Who cares?" said Bushistotle. "I don't have any relatives in the army."

"None of us does, I don't think," said Ashcroftus.

"I'll get our guys in Athens working on it right away," said Rumsfeldiavelli. "Be back in a jiff."

"Okay," said Bushistotle, "but if they can get that plague going, see if you can't find an excuse for keeping us here, ha? Slow down those cedars, 'cause Pasmos is looking better to me every day."

"Consider it done," said Rumsfeldiavelli, who left the briefing room.

No more installments would fit inside of Judith, so I moved onto my next work of art: lucky me, I struck Michelangelo pay dirt again! This time it was his Sistine Chapel version of The Last Judgment, all full of studly nudes headed straight for damnation. I looked among the crowd on their way down to see if I could find a face among them that resembled mine; I was certain that I wasn't going to find a body that resembled mine, but if there was a face, maybe it would portend bad (worse?) things for my future.

But it was not to be: I said before that I don't much resemble Italians, and that hasn't changed. I also said before that it's impossible to render the flat surface of a painting on the roundish surface of an egg, and that hasn't changed, either: the actual painting is flat, and sits behind an altar, but putting a lowly chicken egg behind an alter isn't going to have the same emotional impact as Michelangelo's painting, mostly because the nudes would be so necessarily small. You'd need an ostrich egg or something big like that to give the thing some punch. I did my best nonetheless by painting the whole egg blue—representing sky—with a horizontal line toward the top (arbitrarily chosen as the pointy side of the egg) representing the division between heaven and earth, and a horizontal line toward the bottom (arbitrarily chosen as the not-so-pointy side of the egg) representing the division between earth and you-know-where, plus a few bold kind-of-skin-tone vertical strokes with arrows pointing up or down, to give an indication of which way these poor souls were headed. In my estimation most were headed down, so at least I wouldn't be lonely. Then I inserted my next installment and got ready to move on:

Part 8:

"Honorable Ashcroftus, please close the door," said Cheneyon, and Ashcroftus did. Cheneyon continued: "Honorable Bushistotle, we must get rid of Rumsfeldiavelli."

"But why, Honorable Cheneyon?"

"The war is going poorly," said Cheneyon. "Our domestic agenda is stalled."

"Your point is?"

"Things are looking down."

"True, but can't we put a happy face on it?"

"We need a scapegoat," said Cheneyon.

"Somebody to blame the current situation on?" asked Bushistotle.

"Exactly," said Cheneyon. "You had bad advice."

"You're right, I did," said Bushistotle. "I would have never gotten us into this mess if I hadn't received bad advice."

"Excellent," said Cheneyon.

"Rumsfeldiavelli and his Ministry of War promised an easy victory," said Ashcroftus.

"They did," concurred Cheneyon. "And that we would be hailed as liberators."

"They promised that our WLD's would do the trick," said Bushistotle.

"They did," concurred Cheneyon.

"We had all our hopes pinned on those yellow frogs," said Bushistotle.

"We did," concurred Cheneyon.

"They didn't make proper contingencies for the food chain," said Bushistotle.

"They didn't," concurred Cheneyon.

"Who knew yellow frogs could eat that many gnats?" asked Bushistotle.

"But we should have," answered Cheneyon.

"Or that our locusts would die of boredom, poor things?" asked Bushistotle.

"The jury's still out on the actual cause of death," said Cheneyon, "but we should have made calculations."

"Exactly," said Bushistotle. "Honorable Ashcroftus, what say you?"

"Rumsfeldiavelli is expendable."

"Indeed," said Bushistotle.

"We must secure our domestic and foreign policy agendas," said Ashcroftus.

"Yes," said Bushistotle.

"We must retake Byzantium for the Greek people, and institute Compassionate Republicanism," said Ashcroftus.

I flipped to the next full-color glossy and I nearly fell on the floor: The Transfiguration of Bushistotle, it was called, and it was attributed to Botticelli! Was this pro-Bushistotle conspiracy so vast and widespread that they were even forging art and ascribing it to the Old Masters? Was this art then to be displayed at the Vatican Museum, or perhaps even at the Uffizi? And was Charlemagne actually Bushistotle, as well?

I blew this egg harder than I had blown any egg before (or since, for that matter)—so hard, in fact, that it cracked, and I had to take another egg out of the Styrofoam carton and start all over again. Lucky me, out popped an egg with a blood spot! Should I announce it to see if I'd won a prize, I wondered, or just remain silent and continue my decorating?

Just as I was about to shout "Blood Spot!" Bernie shouted "Okay people!" from the head of the room. "Finish up quickly! Let's see what you've managed to come up with! Who's got the most eggs?"

I certainly didn't have the most eggs, but I knew I had the most important ones. I hurried to finish my picture, then stuffed my next and last installment inside my Bushistotle Transfiguration egg:

Part 9:
Rumsfeldiavelli reentered the briefing room. "I have sent out a dispatch

via rowboat, so we don't have to depend so much on the winds," he announced. "They should arrive in Athens in a few days, and we will know within a week or so whether or not we can use the boil powder."

"Rumsfeldiavelli...," said Cheneyon darkly.

"Uh-oh," Rumsfeldiavelli mumbled.

"This war is not going well," said Cheneyon.

"Things'll pick up, I promise," said Rumsfeldiavelli.

"One of the main purposes of the war was to act as a diversion while we rammed our domestic policy agenda through," said Cheneyon.

"Yes," said Rumsfeldiavelli.

"No!" cried Constantina. "The purpose of the war was to secure Persia's olive oil!"

"That, too," said Rumsfeldiavelli.

"No," said Ashcroftus. "It was to reclaim Byzantium for the gods!"

"We'll discuss the true purpose of the war later," said Cheneyon. "Right now, we need a battlefield victory."

"Yes," said Rumsfeldiavelli.

"We need a victory," said Cheneyon.

"One is coming, I promise," said Rumsfeldiavelli.

"We are bogged down militarily," said Cheneyon.

"We're regrouping," said Rumsfeldiavelli.

"We cannot afford a long, drawn-out engagement: there is a danger of a civil war," said Cheneyon.

"We have another top secret locust breeding program underway," said Rumsfeldiavelli.

"I'm afraid it's too little, too late," said Cheneyon.

"No!" cried Rumsfeldiavelli

"Yes," said Cheneyon. "I'm afraid that the Honorable Bushistotle is going to have to ask for your resignation."

"I am?" asked Bushistotle.

"As we discussed," said Cheneyon.

"Oh, no," said Bushistotle after a pause. "I think I'm going to have to overrule myself on that. It would be bad P.R. If we fire Rummy here people will think we made a mistake, that this was a bad idea, and we certainly can never admit that!"

"The only other option is to claim that the insurgency is in its last throes...," said Cheneyon.

"...and beat a hasty retreat," finished Constantina.

"But that's no fun," said Bushistotle. "We must stay the course so I can

sit in judgment of Saladin for all the world to see. I've changed my mind: Rummy, you're doing a heck of a job!"

"HAIL BUSHISTOTLE!" cried the Coterie. "HAIL BUSHISTOTLE!"

Oh what good work I had done stuffing those many Easter eggs full of the almost-true story of Bushistotle as semi-translated by me! Not to mention my engaging, if not too convincing, Paas-inspired reproductions of Vatican Old Masters, but you do what you can with the limited tools (and talent) you're given. I do admit, however, to taking some license: when I painted <u>The Transfiguration of Bushistotle</u> I added a pair of ass ears to him, which the Inquisition called "branks" and which also seemed entirely suitable; I just hoped that nobody would know it was me!

Sister Penelope escorted me back to my Vice-Presidential Cell that night as usual, locked me in with the crucifix she had attached to her waist. She was no less melancholy than she had been for the past few weeks, and no more inclined to break her vow of silence, either by writing on her hand then spitting and rubbing, or gesticulating in one way or another. Thus the only sound exchanged between us was the clicking of our heels down the long and empty corridors, and the grinding sound of the crucifix as it unlocked and relocked my cell door.

Once inside my cell I found a large chocolate Easter bunny—solid chocolate, too, not the hollow shit!—with a calligraphic note attached that said: "Dear Steve: Happy Bunny Day! Love, Bruno." *There he goes again with the "Love, Bruno" business*, I thought, but at least it meant that we were friends once more, despite his cold treatment of me during our mass egg-blowing orgy. I thought about it a second and concluded that the reason for his coldness was that he really couldn't show his affection for me in front of Bernie, what with the cardinal's checkered past and his strident commitment to out us queers on our asses even if it did mean that most all Catholic priests would be collecting long-term unemployment, and Brother Bruno would be out of a job.

I unwrapped the bunny at once but faced the dilemma I had faced every Easter since childhood: Easter bunnies don't have genitals, so I never know where to start eating. In the end I settled on the long and slender ears as I always do, and munched happily away, washing the chocolate down with some of that fine sacramental Christian Brothers wine that my cell was always stocked full of.

At this point I had no idea how long I'd been locked in the Vatican, but with all the good work I had done for Bruno I figured my sentence might be drawing to a close (and since this book is almost finished, it must have been true!). But I felt I had done a disservice to the world by inventing stories that were favorable to Bushistotle, even if that's what had kept me alive, and I also felt that my sort-of translations of what had almost actually been written in the Windex-soaked ancient texts, the result smuggled out in poorly painted blown Easter eggs, was not enough to clarify the record. Therefore, resolute and wasted on crappy red wine and sweet chocolate bunny ears, I approached the crucifix on my wall and took out the pen, ripped the *Divieto di Usare Telefonini* sign down, and set out to write a better one.

To my at-the-time inebriated way of thinking it wouldn't be enough to finesse the story I was about to write as I had my finessed my translations. No! This time I would have to write a story completely baseless in fact, but since that's what Task Force B.S. had done from the very beginning I felt justified in my fallaciousness. I felt I needed verisimilitude, as well, to make sure that people would believe me, so I took matters into my own hands and decided to write in ancient Greek.

Of course I had less of an idea about how to write ancient Greek than I had of how to translate it, but I'd been looking at all those nonsensical-looking letters for such a long time that I figured I could fake something. Trashed as I was, however, it didn't occur to me that I was writing with a ballpoint pen on A4 copy paper with strips of Scotch tape adhered to the corners, and *Divieto di Usare Telefonini* written in black toner on the other side: most people lose sight of reality when they're overcome with passion, and I was mad as hell at Bushistotle for his lies, and madder still at myself for lending them credence.

Thus I set the stage: a never-happened interview of Bushistotle by a never-lived Persian reporter with the never-existed <u>Persepolis Post</u>, who would ask Bushistotle all the questions that I and millions of other people would never be able to ask:

"Welcome, Honorable Bushistotle," said Farah Fatwah, the Persian reporter.

"Thank you," said Bushistotle.

"Are you nervous?"

"I am never nervous," answered Bushistotle, "because my actions have been right-minded, and righteous."

"Then let us begin. The most serious charge against you has been that of corrupting the youth of Persia. What say you to that?"

"That is most malicious," answered Bushistotle. "I would never corrupt a minor. I don't even know any."

"If I may, Honorable Bushistotle," said Farah Fatwah. "I believe that the nature of the charge of corrupting the youth of Persia resides in your belief in a god of your own making, and teaching our youth that it is true."

"It is true," said Bushistotle.

"And if our people have different ones?"

"In my mind," Bushistotle said, "our different gods are all one in the same."

"I'm sorry?" said Farah Fatwah.

"Our different gods are all one in the same."

"Can you explain what you mean by that?"

"Of course not."

"I see. Now then, we have obtained a copy of your wife's book," Farah Fatwah said, "called <u>Dudley the Donkey Learns a Lesson</u>."

"It was like a Bible to me," said Bushistotle, "until I lost it at Delphi, that is. Fell right out of my hands."

"This copy was provided to us by a faithful reader, someone who calls herself 'Karen the Oracle,' and it is profound."

"That Mrs. Bushistotle!" said Bushistotle proudly. "Truly profound! That's why I miss the wise counsel of <u>Dudley</u>. Can I have your copy? Mrs. Bushistotle is mighty mad at me for losing mine!"

"We shall see," said Farah Fatwah. "But for now, in <u>Dudley</u> I have you quoted as saying, 'But Mrs. Bushistotle, I would think that you knew that our Republican Ideal is "One Nation Under the Gods...."'"

"But that was before my conversion on the road to Byzantium," answered Bushistotle.

"Your conversion?" asked Farah Fatwah.

"Yes, when I was reborn."

"How did it happen?"

"Just before noon, when I was on the outskirts of Byzantium, the Lord appeared before me and said, 'Bushistotle, do my work!'"

"Just like that?"

"Yup."

"And you agreed?"

"What else could I do?"

"What has that meant for you?"

"That's when I realized that all the different gods are one in the same. It's when I changed 'One Nation under the Gods' to 'One Nation under God,' and decided to gloss over the differences."

"Gloss them over?"

"We have more important things to worry about than whether my god's better than your god, which he obviously is. Rather, we must confront the big challenges of our own invention instead of passing them on to future generations."

"Like invading Persia?"

"Right now we're fighting important battles and championing freedom because by expanding liberty we make Athens more secure."

"More secure?" Farah Fatwah questioned. "An insurgency has arisen where none existed, and thousands have been killed and continue to be killed."

"That's their problem," Bushistotle answered, "because we know that freedom is not Athens' gift to the world. Freedom is the Almighty's gift to every man...."

"Who's Almighty?"

"We've discussed that already," Bushistotle said. "All the Almighties are all the same in my mind, so don't interrupt me, please. Now, where was I? I can never remember what Cheneyon tells me to say unless I start it over from the very beginning."

"*Freedom is the Almighty's gift to every man....*"

"...woman, and child in the world, even if it means that thousands of lives have to be lost in the process. That's why we've decided to spread it."

"I see," said Farah Fatwah. "Which Almighty?"

"I told you already, it doesn't matter. Mine, yours, ours, it's all the same, because if there's only one God then my God has to be the same as your gods, even if you don't know it yet. But this crusade isn't about my God, is it?"

"To us Persians it is."

"I think that part of my job when spreading freedom is to convince you that it has nothing to do with the Almighty, and I've been praying for a way to do just that. Remember, anyone in the world who works and sacrifices for freedom has a loyal friend in Athens! Men and women in every culture need liberty like they need food, and water, and air. Everywhere that freedom arrives, humanity rejoices. And everywhere that freedom rings, let tyrants fear. Athens will make sure of that!"

"What if we don't believe you? What if we think Athens is tyrannical?"

"Well then we'll just agree to disagree over it—won't we?—until you come around to my point of view, which is inevitable, since God has spoken directly to me, and not to you."

"Even if I could accept that, Honorable Bushistotle, your plan to expand liberty because your Almighty told you to sounds dangerously Messianic."

"Of course it does."

"But what about here in <u>Dudley</u>, when Mrs. Bushistotle says to you: 'Oh, my Bushistotle, Philosopher-Warrior-King of Athens, you must be very careful, for there is much the gods have said that you will not like!?' You answered 'Nonsense!'"

"I begged her not to publish it, but she did," answered Bushistotle. "I am protecting Athens from danger by being prepared, strong, and steadfast! Vigilance is never easy, you know, and neither is paranoia, but both are always essential, now more than ever. I've done the hard work and made the hard choices required of a Philosopher-Warrior-King in challenging times, and because of my leadership, Athens is strong! Because of my vision, Athens will be even stronger! These are values worthy of a great city-state, and they are values worth fighting for!"

"This is the Bushistotle Doctrine of Preemptive Retaliation?"

"It is."

"And these values, are they worth imposing on others?"

"Yes," Bushistotle said, then he clarified: "What I mean is that we're not imposing ourselves upon the Persians, just dropping by for a friendly visit, you know, to save them from themselves. I have always said that we must not impose our culture or our principles. All we do is point our guns, then we leave it up to you."

"How can you not impose your culture when your army is here?"

"Just for a few dozen years, until the job is done."

"What are those principles that you're not imposing?"

"I have said it before: Timeless values."

"Which are?"

"First, 'One Nation under God,' and second, 'Truth, Goodness, and the Athenian Way.'"

"Just to be clear, then: what you're <u>not</u> imposing upon Persia is 'One Nation under God' and 'Truth, Goodness, and the Athenian Way?'"

"Right. That's what we're not imposing."

"What are you imposing?"

"Oh, nothing."

"Your will?"

"Nothing, really, I assure you! Now let's move on."

"I'd really like to stick with this point for a moment."
"Let's move on."
"I'd...."
"I said, move on!"
"Okay then," Farah Fatwah said. "Moving on...."
"Thank you!"
"Do you believe that your ideals, the ones that you're <u>not</u> imposing, that is, have a literal, eternal and unbending meaning?"
"I don't see how ideals cannot be understood literally, or absolutely. Good is good and bad is bad. That's obvious, no?"
"There is no room for debate in your mind on what is good and what is bad?"
"Absolutely not.
"And you are the guardian of that literal meaning?"
"Who else?"
"And that literal meaning is 'binarialism?'"
"'Bushistotlism,'" Bushistotle corrected.
"Okay, 'Bushistotlism,'" said Farah Fatwah.
"Zero and one, or male and female," said Bushistotle. "Good or bad. Black or white. Dog or cat. Yes or no. Bushistotlism is the basis of our Family Values!" Bushistotle inserted his left index finger in rapid-fire succession into a circle he made with his right index finger and thumb. "This is what we do to the world," he said. "Unite it!"
"Indeed," Farah Fatwah said. "Here in Persia we know your unity well. Nonetheless, you said in your speech to the Persian people that the success of Athens increasingly depends on the success of liberty in other lands, which is why you invaded."
"Absolutely. To topple the evil regime of Saladin and establish freedom, which we've done, and are doing. I believe in freedom!"
"Absolute freedom?"
"Well, you can go too far," Bushistotle said. "There ought to be a limit on freedom."
"What sort of a limit would you establish?"
"I never thought about that," Bushistotle said, "beyond that there should be one. The personal taste, I suppose, of those in power."
"Which would be you?"
"Naturally."
"You are quoted in <u>Dudley the Donkey</u> as saying that you believe everyone should be held responsible for their own personal behavior."

"And I do," said Bushistotle.

"But first you were against nation-building, and then you were for spreading liberty, especially here in Persia. Isn't that contradictory?"

"Not at all," Bushistotle said. "I guess it's just my evolution... Damn! I hate that word!"

"Do you think you owe the Athenian people an apology, then, first for claiming it was bad, and now for claiming it is good?"

"Absolutely not," said Bushistotle. "I have come to learn that if we do not build nations then chaos will reign."

"How long did it take you to come to that conclusion?"

"Several years," said Bushistotle.

"Is it flip-flopping?"

"Absolutely not!" claimed Bushistotle. "It's vision! It's leadership! It's having the courage to do things that nobody in his right mind would do, because you know in your that mind it's the right thing to do! It's following the word of God!"

"Then you're claiming your positions are based on what God said?"

"Of course I am. I believe that what God said is right! It's the natural order of things."

"There were some examples that Mrs. Bushistotle gave you that you disagreed with, such as charging interest on loans."

"Well, I think that's a matter of context, of interpretation."

"I see. Then you do as your God tells you?"

"Absolutely."

"Always?"

"Absolutely."

"Including having slaves?"

"As long as they're from a foreign land."

"Persia?"

"Well...."

"If it were ordained by God?"

"If it was ordained...."

"Eating red meat?"

"There are sacrifices."

"Dacron-polyester blend togas?"

"They don't wrinkle, which is a major plus, but I guess linen is okay."

"Stoning to death of adulterers?"

"Only if the adultery is with your neighbor's wife and not, say, with an oracle."

"Death to insolent children?"

"Absolutely."

"Death to murderers?"

"Absolutely."

"Then would you impregnate your sister-in-law if your brother died childless?"

"Well, I'd lean against it. Mrs. Bushistotle already has me in the doghouse over my mess-up with Karen."

"God has ordained it."

"Really?"

"The penalty for not doing so is death."

"Really?"

"Yes."

"Then if God told me to do that, I guess I'd have to give it a whirl. He-he-he!"

"Good," said Farah Fatwah. *"She's in the next room over."*

WHAM! *Bushistotle*, I thought. *You followed all your own rules, but you're not a saint anymore!*

Oh I was so pleased with myself, so happy to have written this lie! Actually, though, closely read it reveals itself not to be so much of a lie: if you're going to ask others to live by the words of your gods, you can't be choosy when it comes to yourself just because your sister-in-law's a dog! So in my mind the whole Farah Fatwah never-happened interview works from an allegorical perspective, because Farah asked all the right questions that all the people really wanted answered!

Now that I had my genuine original almost-in-ancient-Greek pseudo-manuscript convincingly written in blue ballpoint pen on white A4 bond ready, my next step would be to place it strategically so it would be found by a disingenuous myopic monk, and incorporated by him into the true annals of Bushistotle history. This required an origamical paper-folding feat that was none-too-easy after most of a bottle of wine and a pair of scrumptious chocolate bunny ears, but drunkards are not usually dissuaded by their incapacities since for the most part they're unaware of them, and I was no exception.

My plan was simple: fold once, fold twice, fold three times, then roll this way and that, and attach the resulting miniature manuscript to the back of the fronds still wedged into the crucifix behind Jesus' knees thanks to Palm Sunday, which fronds were due to be collected during the week to be turned into ashes for next year's Ash

Wednesday fête. Said miniature manuscript was therefore bound to be found by whoever collected the fronds for recycling—with luck, a disingenuous myopic monk!—who would of course see its worth (albeit by squinting) and take it straight to the Curia to be reviewed. They, naturally, would deem the miniature manuscript authentic and thereafter it would receive the papal-housekeeping seal of approval, and there goes Bushistotle's canonization, right down the proverbial drain!

More than pleased with myself and ready to give in to my fetish, I started eating my bunny's feet. I was half standing above the credence table where I had done all my writing that night, when I heard the lock on my door screwing open. I turned, and there was Sister Penelope standing in the frame; she inched forward, then that same gaggle of old-fashioned nasty Catholic-School nuns who pack holsters stuffed with steel rulers for whacking you across the knuckles on, just in case you get out of line, rushed into my cell and grabbed hold of me and my origamically miniature manuscript.

"Hey, watch it!" I slurred. "You're gonna mess up my genuine authentic mini-manuscript that I just wrote!"

Hell, was I toasted!

Then Sister Naomi shuffled in, mumbled "achim sadoc abiud amon zorobabel" to me again, which this time I dared not reflate back into English since as her Instant Messages had shown I'd gotten all my past reflations so horribly wrong.

Sister Naomi held up a sheet of parchment: from what I could see (which wasn't much) it was none other than "The Temptation of Bushistotle" story that I had stashed under the silver tray containing my Eucharist hors d'oeuvres that I figured no one would ever pick up, which she must have found while cleaning. Sister Naomi looked at me and shook her head no, and Sister Penelope did the same. Then Sister Penelope motioned for the gaggle of nuns to hustle me out of the room, which they did.

Nuns are a pushy lot, let me tell you, but they're especially pushy when they're rushing to get you to the Inquisition; in no time at all I was hustled through miles of hall and found myself again inside the walnut-paneled office of Cardinal Bernie, wherein off to one side was the door that led to the safe that led to Task Force B.S., through which I had once been escorted as a guest of honor at the invitation of the pope.

Not this time, though: Bernie was sitting at his oversized desk; Bruno was standing beside him. Mrs. Irma R. Gorgonzola was off to the other side, and Sister Penelope took a place behind her. Sister Naomi shuffled back and forth, constantly mumbling "achim sadoc abiud amon zorobabel," until she found herself next to Bruno, though she still continued to mumble "achim sadoc abiud amon zorobabel." The other nuns in the gaggle formed a black-robed crescent behind me, blocking my access to the door.

"Good evening, Stevie-boy," said Bernie.

"Good evening, Bernie," I said.

"Your Eminence, now," Cardinal Lei said.

"Your Eminence," I repeated humbly.

"Hello, Steven," said Bruno.

"Thanks for the chocolate bunny," I responded.

"Chocolate bunny?" Cardinal Lei said. He turned to Bruno. "And what's that all about?"

"Not to worry," Bruno said. "There's nothing between us. It was part of the plan."

Nothing between us? I thought. *Nothing between us. Oh my God! Bruno and Bernie are homoousians!* But I said nothing, since silence seemed the best response.

Bruno bent down behind the cardinal's desk, arose holding a brown-and-yellow basket full of Easter eggs resting on a surfeit of green plastic grass. "These are yours?" he enquired.

At the distance I stood it was difficult for me to see whether the Paas paintings on the eggshells were indeed mine, but I figured that if Bruno was holding them up asking me that question, then he already knew the answer. "Quite possible," I answered. "Is my art bad?"

"Radical," Bruno said, "especially the branks." Then he dumped the production of my egg-blowing orgy onto the floor, and almost all of the shells cracked open. Sister Naomi immediately started to pick up the green plastic grass and the eggshells, but Cardinal Lei stopped her.

"Hand me an unbroken egg!" he commanded in a booming voice, and Sister Naomi complied. Cardinal Lei fondled it in what I would characterize as an inappropriate manner for an adult with a defenseless egg, then he extracted my onionskin paper from it and crushed the shell in his hand. "What have we here?" he asked insidiously, and most definitely rhetorically.

"Cigarette paper?" I answered. "For a joint?"

"Funny," the cardinal said. He unrolled the paper and began to read:

Part 1: Notwithstanding the technological superiority of the Athenian Armed Forces, Bushistotle's war is not going well: Saladin's capture has turned him into a martyr, and an insurgency has been born that threatens the stability of Byzantium, this because, unforeseen by the Athenian philosophers at the time they declared war, the Persians were not quite as keen to accept 'Truth, Goodness and the Athenian Way' as they had figured. Volunteers are pouring into Byzantium from all the many provinces of Persia, and threaten to overwhelm the Coalition forces. Casualties have been high."

"What is this?" the cardinal asked me.

"The true history of Bushistotle?" I asked.

"NO!" the cardinal boomed. "It is BLASPHEMY! APOCRYPHA!" He then picked up a page from his desk, and read it: "*A great and thankful multitude had come to watch the Investiture of Bushistotle as Emperor of Persia. With the help of a timber multinational to which Bushistotle's Interior Department had recently granted harvesting rights throughout Anatolia and the Levant, including the near-extinct cedars of Lebanon, the multitude took copious amounts of palm fronds that had been destined for pulping; they set them down upon the road as Bushistotle proceeded toward the Imperial Palace.*

"*The multitude cried out: 'Hosanna! Blessed is He who comes in the name of the Greeks!'*"

It was the story I had invented on Bushistotle's entry into Byzantium, to please Task Force B.S. "That," Cardinal Lei said, "is the true story of Bushistotle, the one that will be disseminated among the people!"

"But I made that story up," I protested, perhaps stupidly.

"NONSENSE!" shouted Cardinal Lei. "Hail Bushistotle!"

All the others in the room joined with him, except Sister Mary Subjugation, owing, I suppose to her vow of silence: "Hail Bushistotle! Hail Bushistotle!" In Sister Naomi's case it sounded more like "achim sadoc abiud amon zorobabel," and in Mrs. Irma R. Gorgonzola's more like "Hail a Bushistotele a!" but you get the point: I was vastly outnumbered.

"There is an orthodoxy that we follow here in the Vatican," Cardinal Lei said. "And when the facts don't agree with the orthodoxy something has to suffer, and what suffers are the facts. We must portray Bushistotle in the best light possible!"

"And damn the truth?" I asked.

"And damn the truth!" Cardinal Lei responded.

"Spartans are Persians and Persians are Spartans," I answered.

"Enough!" Cardinal Lei said. "There were Spartans in Persia, even if there weren't. I tire of you."

"But I was only following Bruno's orders," I said.

Bruno smiled evilly, and winked at me. "Don't you think we have to test the loyalty of our fellow Task Force B.S. members before we can trust them?"

"I was set up?"

Fra Diavolo smiled evilly. "I don't like to be spurned," he answered.

Cardinal Lei motioned to Sister Mary Subjugation, who handed him the folios containing "The Temptation of Bushistotle." "What is this blasphemy?" the cardinal asked me.

"I didn't write it, I swear!" I pleaded. "I found it beneath my copy of Bushistotle's 'I'm-reluctant-to-declare-war-but-gee-I-have-to' speech. I've read it, but I am not the author."

"You expect me to believe that after the sacrilegious story you stuffed in the Easter eggs? You expect people to believe that Bushistotle fucked with an oracle?"

"There are numerous references throughout the historical record, including in Bushistotle's genealogy!" I cried. "There are numerous references stating that the oracle said one thing in the heat of passion—'My son, thou art invincible'—that Bushistotle interpreted incorrectly!"

Cardinal Lei motioned to Mrs. Irma R. Gorgonzola, who handed him an ancient volume. "Do you know what this is?" the cardinal asked.

"No idea," I answered.

"It is the last existing copy of <u>Dudley the Donkey Learns a Lesson</u>."

"Could I have it?" I asked. "I'd love to see what it says!"

"Silence!" Cardinal Lei shouted. "We have compared it to your blasphemous writings, and we find in it none of the quotations you attribute to Mrs. Bushistotle!"

I feigned surprise: "Really?"

"You don't speak ancient Greek, do you, Steve?" the cardinal asked.

"Well...."

"Your website was a lie!"

"Well...."

"You made this entire story up!"

"But that's what Task Force B.S. is doing!"

"But that is toward a greater good: proclaiming Bushistotle to be the Messiah, put here on earth to save mankind from itself. Hail Bushistotle!"

"Hail Bushistotle!" the crowd cried, with the same caveats as before. "Hail Bushistotle!"

Cardinal Lei took a very long and deep breath, then laid back in his comfortable looking crimson leather chair: with his cardinal's duds on he practically camouflaged in. "I am done with you, Steven," he finally announced. "Done with you. Unfortunately, you shall suffer the fate of all your predecessor ancient Greek translators."

I asked, "Which is?" even though I knew the answer.

Mrs. Irma R. Gorgonzola made a slicing motion across her neck with her finger, and I recalled: how far is Sicily from Rome?

There was a momentary lapse of silence, then Cardinal Lei announced: "*Unde multos combussimus et adhuc cum invenimus idem facere non cessamus.*" He flicked his wrist and the crescent of black-robed nuns encircled me, and immediately hustled me back to my cell. This time, however, it was not the Vice-Presidential Cell replete with a partial view, stale Eucharist hors d'oeuvres, tasty Christian Brothers sacramental wine and a wall-mounted crucifix with a secret compartment plus the tasty remains of my solid chocolate Easter bunny, but rather my original dingy cell with a bedpan and no view, and a *Divieto di Usare Telefonini* sign posted to the wall. If only I had a *telefonino* I could have called for help, but I was still the only one in

Italy without one. Someday, I hoped, cell phone technologies would converge.

But that was not the case, and I was incommunicado again, locked in and awaiting what I was certain would be my execution at dawn, probably right after Matins, since it's been proved historically that executions are always best after right after prayer. Truth is, I'd always known I would die but preferred not to admit it, but I never thought I would die like this! I recalled some of the Inquisition's favorite modes of murder—burning at the stake (ouch!), garrotes (gasp!), beheading (oops!), drawing and quartering (heeeeeeelp!)—when my mind filled with these words: *Corrigi eos volumus, non necari, nec disciplinam circa eos negligi volumus, nec suppliciis quibus digni sunt exerceri.*

I have no idea what that means, but then of course I had no idea what any of the texts I had "translated" actually meant, either. (Ακαδημια? Please!) I was cool with that, but with death now staring me in the face I was certain to my core of just one thing: never again in my life would I answer an unsolicited email from Rome!

I lay on the uncomfortable cot for what seemed like hours, tried to stay warm under the Alitalia blanket, tried to rest my head on the tiny Alitalia pillow, but I was never able to fall asleep on a plane. I tossed, turned, and for the first and last time in my life I wished I had a nice big jug of Christian Brothers wine: facing death is so much easier when you're obliterated out of your mind. I thought that if I hadn't been so prejudiced against the tonsured look, perhaps Fra Diavolo wouldn't have betrayed me. But then of course there was no way to know that, or exactly what his relationship to Cardinal Lei was: could a gay man really think that Bushistotle was the Savior, too?

At what time of night I do not know, I heard a crucifix being inserted into the lock on my door. I stood to see what was happening, and the door creaked open. Sister Mary Subjugation was standing in front of me. "At midnight," she said, "come out into the hall. Do not tarry." Then she closed the door but did not lock it, and I heard her footsteps fleeing down the hall.

I was dumbstruck: she had spoken to me and broken her vows. But was it another trap? Could she be believed? If I stepped outside at midnight would I be confronted with the long and pointy pikes of the Vatican Swiss Guard, or perhaps the machine gun rat-tat-tats of Bushistotle terrorists? I knew that Task Force B.S. was vicious in their methods, and would go to all lengths to ensure that their orthodox line be toed; truth suffered in the name of expediency, and words to them had no meaning. If I had committed a sin, however, it was merely to use their tactics against them—or was my sin the fact that I'd been caught?

In the end I decided I had no choice but to follow Sister Mary Subjugation's order; precisely at midnight—or at least more or less at midnight—I for the first time opened my cell door on my own, and stepped out into the hall. I looked left and saw nothing; I looked right and saw nothing. I looked left, right, left, right, but always saw nothing.

Then, "*Pssst!*" in the distance.

It was dark, but I looked.

"*Pssst!*"

It was Sister Naomi, and she waved at me to approach her!

My heart fluttered—was I really going to get out?—and I raced to where she was standing, at the head of an ancient staircase. "Can you get me out of here, Sister?" I asked, and she answered "*Sì, posso.*"

"What?" I said. "Not 'achim sadoc abiud amon zorobabel?'"

"*Achim, Sadoc, Abiud, Amon, Zorobabel: che merda!*"

"'Achim, Sadoc, Abiud, Amon, Zorobabel: what shit!?'" I repeated, questioning.

"*Che merda!*" she repeated. "*Bushistotele, figlio di Dio! Che classe di merda! Allora seguimi, e fa' presto!*"

I followed her orders and followed her quickly. We raced down several flights of stairs, when suddenly, there was a body: Sister Mary Subjugation—I means Sister Penelope—face down with her feet toward the top of the stairs, a knife in her hand, her wrist sliced and a river of blood oozing down the marble steps! Her cell phone was several steps below her, lying like Captain Kirk's phaser after he's been struck by an evil Romulan.

What an allegory! I thought, but my Italian wasn't nearly good enough to explain American pop culture to Sister Naomi, so instead I cried, "Sister Penelope!"

"*Lasciala stare!*" Sister Naomi ordered. "*È morta.*"

"She's dead?!"

"*Suicida!*"

Again I followed orders, left poor Sister Penelope to bleed to death on the stairs; Sister Naomi shuffled down one further flight, where at the landing there was a statute of a naked man. *Nice*, I thought, then much to my surprise Sister Naomi reached up and tickled his testicles—she'd probably been wanting to do that for years!—and the statue slid to one side, revealing a tunnel. She pushed me in, and the statue closed behind us.

It was pitch dark, but on the wall was a flashlight, and Sister Naomi turned it on. We descended further and further down, and in my mind it was growing increasingly warm, but the truth is the temperature remained cool. Soon we reached the end of the tunnel, and Sister Naomi banged on the wall. It slid open, and we were inside Mrs. Irma R. Gorgonzola's office again.

Irma was standing before me, holding a book. She handed it to me. "Dis a bee a dee a true a history of a Bushistotele a," she mangled. "Dee a Windex *versione*, itta bee a fake a! Now a go a!"

Mrs. Irma R. Gorgonzola rushed toward the dusty oversized St.-Francis-of-Assisi-holding-a-vicious-looking-squirrel-in-his-arms statue that was in the corner, pressed the squirrel's left eye, and the statue moved to one side, revealing a ladder-in-a-hole underneath. Sister Naomi descended first. I was about to follow, but hesitated: I didn't know whether to thank Mrs. Irma R. Gorgonzola for rescuing me—if I was indeed being rescued!—or to scream at her for putting me through so much torture. In the end I said, "Could I have that last copy of <u>Dudley the Donkey Learns a Lesson</u>, too, for posterity purposes?"

"Itta bee a wit a dee a *cardinale*," she said. "But itta bee a bunch a of a B. a S. a, too a!"

"I figured," I said, and descended the ladder as St.-Francis-of-Assisi-holding-a-vicious-looking-squirrel-in-his-arms covered the hole above me. I reached the bottom, where it was dark again, but Sister Naomi, huffing and puffing, held the flashlight bravely and marched us forward.

"Where are you taking me?" I asked her.

"*Alla libertà*," she answered. "*Fuori del Vaticano, a Roma.*"

"And this book?" I asked, questioning her about the book that Mrs. Irma R. Gorgonzola had given me.

"*È la verità*," she said, "*intorno a Bushistotele.*"

"The truth about Bushistotle?"

She stopped a moment, and I could see that she was fatigued; she could barely breathe now. "*Aprilo*," she said. "*Aprilo*."

So I opened the book and read, and to my amazement I saw my own English sort-of translations of Bushistotle that I had basically made up, translated right back into ancient Greek and forged on parchment to make them look original. "I wrote this," I said.

"*Sì, lo so*," Sister Naomi answered: she knew!

Sister Naomi faltered, and I helped her; our pace slowed but we made our way through the tunnel. Then, at the end, an ancient iron gate on the other side of which was a grotto. Sister Naomi took the crucifix that was attached to her waist, opened the gate. "*Il mio crocifisso lo apre tutto*," she said. "*Fu un dono da Giovanni XXIII*."

I entered the grotto; Sister Naomi followed. "Can't Brother Bruno find us in these tunnels?" I asked.

"*Tutte le gallerie e grotte che conosce lui sono vicoli ciechi*," she said.

"All dead ends?"

"*Sì*."

"*Andiamo, poi*," I said: "Let's go now."

Sister Naomi sat on a rock ledge. "*Non vado più*," she said, now gasping for air. "*Siamo nelle catacombe. Qui nacqui, qui muoio. Chiudi il cancello*."

She was willingly giving her life for mine—or for the Truth, of which I was merely the vessel—so I obeyed: I closed the iron gate and it locked of its own; Sister Naomi handed me the flashlight and pointed me in the proper direction, and I left her in the catacombs to die. I walked and walked and walked, and the flashlight grew dim, and I held the forged truth I had written about Bushistotle close my chest, until in the distance I saw a light. And there I ascended from the catacombs holding what the world would one day know as the true history of Bushistotle as invented by me, and I came out into the bright sun of Rome. Now smelling freedom for the first time in a long time I sat on a bench, and reflected. In the end I concluded that despite the hardship, despite the pain, and despite the 30 or so pounds gained, I was pleased with my accomplishment: during my imprisonment in the Vatican I had managed to tell the truth about Bushistotle by telling nothing but bald-faced lies, whereas Task Force B.S. had only managed to tell lies about Bushistotle by telling even more bald-faced lies. Which, to you, is the greater literary achievement?

ABOUT THE AUTHOR

Steven Hanley holds a Master's degree in Spanish literature from Columbia University. He has lived in London, Madrid and Singapore, speaks Spanish and Portuguese, and has traveled extensively throughout the world. On his mother's side he is descended from the Vanderbilts, but unfortunately for him he was disinherited when his wealthy great-grandmother ran off with the circus. On his father's side his family has been traced to a group of 48 Albanian soldiers who in 1490 bravely fled the advance of the Ottoman Turks to Sicily, where they lived in abject poverty for over 400 years, until relocating to public housing in Queens circa 1940. Steve, however, prefers Manhattan.